Understanding Money

Rod Moon

Understanding Money

Rod Moon

Nordberg Press

Waterford, Michigan

ISBN: 0984819428

Printed in the United States of America

"[7] The rich rule over the poor,
and the borrower is slave to the lender."

Proverbs 22:7

Contents

What is Money?

In an exhaustive search for knowledge, we have gone so far as to ask the "man on the street" for the answer to, what is money?
Here are the incredible responses obtained by this research:

First person, "Go away! I am not going to give you any money. Go on, get out of here!"

Second person, "It's what you never have enough of and can't have too much of."

Third person, "Ah yes, money, what indeed, yes, ah, the root of all evil, what makes the world go round, follow the money and find the answer to every other question you have, money can't make you happy, but sure makes you comfortable in your misery. Wait, there's more."

Fourth person, "You're kidding? Dig your hand in your pocket, it's those bills and coins you find there. What are you, some kind of idiot? Dollars and cents, you numbskull."

Fifth person, "The stuff the government makes and then takes away from you."

We then conferred with the eminent and well-known economic expert Doctor Noah Tolle, PhD, PDQ, ADD. Who assures us of the exact meaning of money from his vast knowledge on the subject. Here the great mind is quoted saying,

> "Significant progenitors of the efficacy on which market modems generate standard variation toward, linear, or exponential, expansion, or decline from central fiscal diverse and derivative function, as specified within marginal concomitant usage seen in the degree of notation."

We were unable to understand any of that, so we asked a guy who ran a business here in Detroit. He gave an interesting answer. He said that money is what people use to make doing business easier.

Since the first people began trading things that they wanted from each other they used common trade items to make it easy. Maybe they didn't have enough hides or cloth to get all the food they wanted, so they traded a common item of agreed value instead. Unusual

shells were used, or pearls, and especially gold and silver because these were rare and hard to find. In Bible times pearls were very valuable. Gold and silver had a special ability to be melted and then harden into any shape. Governments quickly learned to mold them into coins. The face of the king or Emperor went on to the face of the coins to identify their origin.

Leviticus 27:25 says that *"Every value is to be set according to the sanctuary shekel, twenty gerahs to the shekel."* Gerah, just means 1/20 of a shekel. The shekel was gold first used in 3000 B.C.

The earliest shekels were a unit of metal weight traded before the advent of coins. Early traders stamped coins to avoid weighing them each time used. The value could be recognized on sight. The ancient historian Herodotus states that the first coinage was issued by Croesus King of Lydia, leading to the golden shekel, issued by the Persian Empire, and then the Silver, Greek drachma. A gold shekel continued in use in the city state of Tyre and later Carthage, 300 B.C. as seen in the Carthaginian coin shown here.

Roman money during most of the Roman Republic and Empire consisted of coins including the **aureus**, a gold coin, the **denarius**, a silver coin, the **sestertius**, a brass coin, and copper coins too. These were used for six hundred years, from the middle of the third century BC until the middle of the third century AD.

Here are several coins used by the Romans. Note that each has a weight. A person trading goods or services

COMMON COINS OF THE ROMAN EMPIRE

A free infographic by *Dirty Old Coins, LLC*

for these coins would know at a glance the value of what they received. Even outside the empire these coins would retain their value because of the value of the metal from which they were made. The markings made the coins valuable too. People learned their value, or "buying power" both within and outside the empire.

Money changers in ancient cities specialized in buying and selling coins from different parts of the world. For a small percentage they would take coins from anywhere in trade for the local money. These exchanges were based on the value of the coins by determining the weight of the metal from which they were made.

Every place on earth through history has had known values for gold, silver, copper, and brass. Coins that could not be exchanged because the country they came from was too remote could still be melted to make local money or traded for their metal weight value.

The ancient world did not print paper currency because they did not have printing presses. Individuals did write notes by hand promising payment. These promissory notes were always redeemed for precious metal coins.

Only coins have **intrinsic** value, meaning a **value of their own**.

To understand money, one must understand "troy weight". **Troy weight** is a system of units of mass used for precious metals and gemstones. Troy weight is always measured in ounces.

Troy weight probably takes its name from the French market town of **Troyes, in France**, where foreign merchants traded at least as early as the 9th century A.D.

One troy ounce is equal to just a **bit over 31 Grams.** This is more than the standard ounce weight of 28.4 grams.

A **Troy pound** is **12 Troy ounces.**

The British, set the **pound sterling** as their main coin many centuries ago, it is valued at **one Troy Pound.** Note that the British Pound has always been a coin.

A **Troy** ounce of silver is **€28.50 Euros** in 2024.
Or **$28.61 US** in 2024.
Or **£23.64 British Pounds** in 2024.

Money for many centuries has been coins made from precious metals. These coins could be traded easily between foreign countries because their **intrinsic** value did not change with time, war, borders, or rulers. In fact, the exchange of foreign and U.S. Coins dominated business in the United States until the Civil War. The first American coins were struck in 1793.

So, what, you may ask, is the printed paper people call money? It is <u>not</u> money! It is used in place of money.

The use of paper goes back to those notes individuals would write promising to pay someone for goods or services. They would put the amount on the paper, the name of the person to get the money and sign the paper to verify it.

When governments and banks got printing presses, after 1439, they began to make notes promising to pay money that was not ready at hand. The notes specified an amount giving a certification and signature. Anyone with the note could redeem them for precious metal coins from the government or bank.

Some governments decided to print a lot of paper notes to cover debts. The American Government during the revolution printed so many they became worthless. After all, they were not money. Money is precious metal, made into marked coins to assure its weight. This is why in 1787 the Constitution gave Congress to power to "**coin**" money, not print it.

The American dollar used to look like this one here.

It's made of silver and has intrinsic value anywhere in the world. See the little marks all around the edge, called "**reeds**". Those aren't just decorations, like on your Aunt Martha's pie. Those reeds are there to assure the coin's weight.

Centuries ago, the Roman government tried to save money by cutting tiny chunks off the edges of their coins which they melted to make more coins. People got wise about the fact that the coins were getting lower in weight. They raised prices to make up for the loss in value.

Those decorative marks, or reeds, at the edge of coins keep anyone from making "money on the side".

When President Jackson eliminated the Central bank in 1833, state banks began printing notes for business use. Counterfeiters easily copied these notes. Panicked businessmen made huge demands for coins the banks could not meet, resulting in a large number of bank failures.

During the Civil War the U.S. created over $400 million in printed paper certificates to finance its war. These were called "**greenbacks"** because of the green

tinge of the print. The government backed this currency with a promise that it could be used to pay back public and private debts. The value fluctuated according to the North's fortunes in the war.

Currency is the proper name for paper showing promised value, but it is not money. Currency does not have intrinsic value. Money, coins made from precious metals have intrinsic value. People do like to have currency. That is because it is so widely accepted for buying stuff.

The U.S. Government continued to issue "greenbacks" after the Civil War and issued "**Silver Certificates**" like this in the 20th century.

See what it says,
"One Silver Dollar, Payable to the Bearer on Demand."

This certifies that one dollar, in silver deposited in the treasury of the United States must be paid to anyone in exchange for this paper dollar. If you find one of these hang on to it.

The government now issues **Federal Reserve notes.**

See what it says across the top of this bill.

The difference between a **Silver Certificate** and a **Federal Reserve Note** is that a Federal Reserve note cannot be redeemed for coins. It is **Fiat currency.** The term <u>fiat</u> comes from Latin, meaning "let it be done," by decree. It has no intrinsic value.

Fiat currency derives its value from a government promise. Fiat money originated in 11th century China. It was first used in America by the Continental congress. The fiat Continental dollars quickly became worthless because people knew they had nothing of value backing them.

When the U.S. Constitution was written, it provided congress had the sole power to "**coin money**". The founders wanted no more printing press dollars that become worthless because they have no intrinsic value. The desperate government of the Civil War reversed that part of the constitution, without an amendment, by making the claim of backing the dollar with precious metal.

Today US Federal Reserve notes have no material backing. They are backed, the Federal Reserve says, **"by the full faith and power of the U.S. Government."**

After World War II, in 1945, America became the principal financial power of the world. At an agreement of all the major financial powers, at **Bretton Woods, these countries decided to base international banking on the U. S. Dollar. A dollar, at the time, backed by substantial gold reserves.**

Rapidly growing U.S. debt in 1970 led to a crisis. The amount of U.S. gold able to be exchanged for the paper dollar declined from 55% to 22%. Foreign holders of the U.S. dollar lost faith in the U.S. government's ability to stop printing dollars, to cut its budget, and its trade deficits. **These countries began to refuse the US dollar, demanding debts be paid in gold.**

The dollar dropped in value against European currencies. Switzerland withdrew the Swiss Franc from the Bretton Woods System. Other countries were sure to follow the Swiss in short order.

President Richard Nixon ended the direct exchange of United States Dollars for precious metal to stop the loss of gold from our treasury. Since then, all US currencies have been **fiat currencies**.

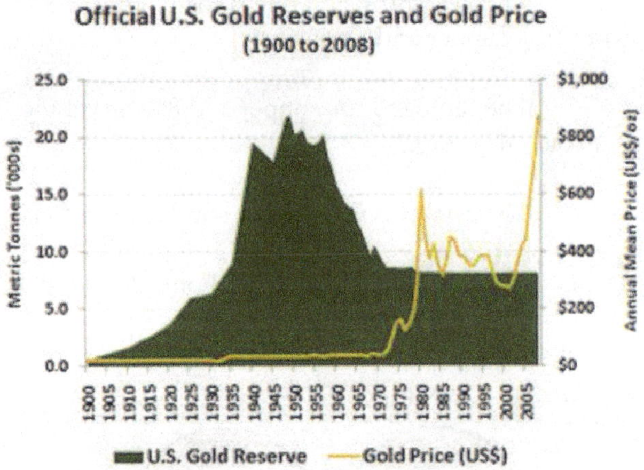

The Euro is also a fiat currency. Every country in the world now operates on fiat currency.

President Nixon's action ended the emergency. Today the U.S. still holds the greatest gold reserves in the world. Most of that gold is in New York City, but we do not own it.

The danger of any fiat currency is that it is at the mercy of man's perception and intentions, both good and evil. This has caused fiat currencies around the world to vary wildly in value.

The stuff in your pocket is not money. Money must have **intrinsic value** to avoid the unpredictable antics of mankind.

The coins you use are made with little precious metal. You can find more silver in your cell phone or computer than in your change, even if your pocket is filled with coins.

The best intrinsic value is the quarter, made with 91% copper and 8% nickel.

The dime is 91% copper and 8% nickel too but has little weight.

The Nickel is 75% copper and 25% nickel.

The penny is 97% zinc and only 2% copper.

It costs almost two cents per coin to mint one penny.

Wealth and Abundance

It has been a claim ever since political speech began that the rich need to pay their "fair share." No one has ever described what a fair share is exactly. No one has even suggested what a fair share of one's income might be.

Neither has anyone explained how a government tax break "gives" people money. Tax breaks are also known as tax concessions, or tax relief, a reduction of payments by taxpayers. How does that "give" taxpayers money. Income belongs to the taxpayer not the government. Government usually applies tax breaks to stimulate the economy, increase the wealth of the population. Again, where is the gain? Doesn't the tax money come from the people in the first place?

Take a ten-dollar bill, put it in your right pocket, then move it to your left pocket. Have you increased your wealth? Yet the government claims it will take money from one group of people, move it to another group of people and claim wealth increased. One group lost, one group gained. Where is the additional money?

There has been a lot of government talk about wealth redistribution to improve the economy The government cannot increase wealth by taking money away from people. All they can do is redistribute it.

Understanding what wealth is and how it is created is essential to seeing through the false notion of redistributing money.

The concept of wealth comes from understanding of abundance. Abundance of any commodity, either a product or service, represents wealth. An abundance of any commodity can always be converted into money. An abundant crop of wheat, an abundant supply of mined minerals, abundant machined parts, all represent wealth.

Notice that abundance is produced only by labor. ***The wealth* of the world comes from the labor of human hands**. It cannot be created in any other way. For a person, a city, or a country to be wealthy requires the labor of human hands. Even a country that makes wealth from mining alone needs miners. Abu Dhabi makes money from oil alone. Someone must drill down, coax it out of the sand, put it in barrels, refine it and ship it; all that is labor of human hands.

In any business, the first to benefit from the business are the workers, not the business owners. Since the business must first produce its product or service before it can enjoy a profit, the workers must be paid before the profit is made.

In the case of Amazon.com, which went into business in 1994, there were no profits until 2001. During those seven years workers had to be paid.

Some people gain wealth from the sale of products, some from the sale of real estate, some by lending money, and others inherit money from their parents. Still, **all wealth originates from the labor of human hands.** There are no products, real estate or money to lend without labor first. That fact must be thoroughly grasped to understand economics.

This rudimentary fact gets lost in the hodgepodge of economic terms floated by governments and economists bent on hiding where wealth really comes from. Economists shroud it in a labyrinth of technical phrases. Anyone claiming that wealth can be achieved by some method other than labor creating abundance is deceiving.

Not everyone can own a mine, a farm, a factory, or a fishing boat, to produce an abundance. Some will have to live by working for those that do. Some people will always be wealthier than others. Christ assures us that the poor will always be with us.

How the wealth gets distributed falls to chance and cleverness. Wealth and abundance are fickle friends staying in one place and moving suddenly to another. There is no guarantee of getting wealth or keeping it. The best one can do is to take great care in money matters.

The top 1% of the wealthiest people in America are only in the top 1% briefly.

Only 13% of the top 1% will remain there for more than one year.

Those not wealthy must to some degree be dependent on those who are wealthy for their livelihood. As wealth grows so does the size of the group that the wealthy support.

It makes no sense to limit or impede the growth of wealth. The growth of business wealth leads to the growth of the whole community: labor, housing, services and infrastructure. It does this because a business will have ships, farms, factories, and stores at which work is found. In turn those workers spend money throughout the community to provide their needs.

The inverse is also true. When the wealth of business declines owners cut spending and reduce the labor force. The whole community suffers to some degree.

Abundance always invests in more growth when free to do so. It thrives best in a lower tax environment and produces more government revenue at lower tax rates.

When business owners are free to make money under limited taxes and regulations they can prosper. That prosperity is seen first by workers through wages. Eventually the business owner may reap a profit, but there is no guarantee, the statistics of failed businesses attest to the risks an owner takes.

Neither do the wealthy sit on their money, they invest it, boosting the economy and increasing the wealth of other businesses, in turn prospering everyone. The growth of industry during the late 19th and early 20th century did exactly that, benefiting the common worker first, then the business.

In 1900 the average American worker earned $700.00 a year. There were no paid vacations, holidays, or sick leave. A laborer worked and got paid or did not work and did not get paid.

During the decade from 1910 to 1920 the average worker's salary increased to $1,500 a year. By the late 1920s more than 60% of Americans were making $2,000 to $2,500 a year, with added benefits and paid vacation time. All of this resulted from business that thrived during that period.

Economic growth in the 1920s in the United States was called the "Roaring Twenties." A period of increase in **consumer spending** because of higher income. This led to innovations in production and advertising. Many household items became more affordable, allowing families to enjoy a higher standard of living. Look at what one could buy for one dollar in the 1920s:

Three gallons of gasoline
Two meals at a restaurant
Eight loaves of bread
One whole chicken
Three pounds of hamburger
Four pounds of ham
Two men's suits
One record, the latest in recordings at the time.

There are about 6 million small businesses in the United States. Small businesses employ an estimated 73% of workers. Large employing businesses, with over 1,000 workers, provide about 42% of all jobs.

A bit fewer than half of small businesses have just one to four workers, according to estimates from the Census Bureau. Just 1% of small businesses have between 100 to 499 workers.

The 6 million small businesses will generate about $16 trillion per year. Small businesses with more employees tend to account for larger shares of overall revenue than those with fewer workers.

Companies with less than 100 employees typically make less than 4 million dollars in sales yet are considered wealthy because they are employers.

Any additional expense falling upon these smaller companies is quickly reflected on their employees, and on what those employees can buy. When those firms suffer their employees feel it immediately. Employees find nothing theoretical in being deprived of their income.

The money they don't spend is keenly felt by retail establishments throughout their community.

Since wealth comes only from labor, and growing wealth creates opportunities for additional labor, it is desirable to have wealth grow.

For there to be wealthy people, there must first be workers who benefit from wages before that wealth is created, if the risks can be overcome. In the meantime, the worker is paid whether the business survives or not.

Scarcity and Choice

One of the bedrock principles of economics is scarcity. Thomas Sowell teaches that:

"Economics is the study of the use of scarce resources which have alternative uses."

Yes, we just learned about wealth and abundance related to economics, but scarcity must be understood to truly grasp this subject. There are just two things that can be exchanged for money: labor and property. Those two things are not always available in the amount desired. This causes people to make choices based on what is available.

In Michigan, because we are by the Great Lakes, water is abundant. In the desert southwestern states water is limited, scarce. It causes both the use and cost of water to be different in each area.

To some degree all goods and services are limited. A business hiring workers may find it hard to fill certain jobs that require special skills. That fact may affect the amount of pay offered for those positions. Higher pay may be offered to overcome the scarcity of specialized workers. If the employer cannot afford to pay more for labor an alternative solution must be found.

When a hot new Christmas gift becomes a massive hit, if the manufacturer does not anticipate the high demand there won't be enough product for the customers. Prices for copycat gifts from similar producers might skyrocket. People wanting to buy the hot new gift might have to choose an alternative.

Scarcity and choice are directly related to supply and demand. **Supply** being how much of a commodity is available. **Demand** is how much of the commodity is wanted. When **supply** and **demand** are in balance, prices tend to stay stable. When one of these outweigh the other, prices go up or down depending on the circumstances. The **law of supply and demand** is a fundamental concept in economics that explains how prices are determined in an economy.

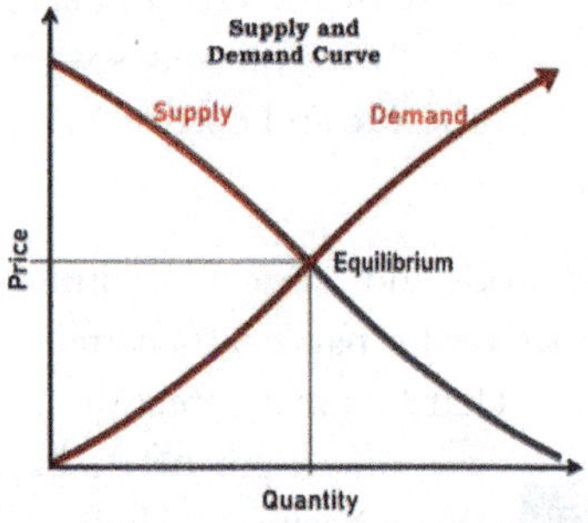

This relationship can be represented by a simple graph known as the supply and demand curve. The supply curve shows the quantity of a product that suppliers are willing to sell at different prices, while the demand curve shows the quantity that consumers are willing to buy at different prices.

On the demand side, consumer needs and preferences, product cost, and the level of competition can all impact the demand for a product or service. On the supply side, factors such as production limits, raw material availability, labor shortage, and government regulations can affect the quantity of goods and services that are available. These factors can cause customers and producers to seek alternative choices.

Making a choice, picking an alternative, means giving up something to gain something else. This is a constant situation in economics referred to as **opportunity cost**.

An opportunity cost could be money, product or time. Every decision involves separate alternatives making opportunity cost inevitable in a world of limited resources.

When a business invests in new equipment, the opportunity cost is the potential return from the investments the business did not choose.

When one spends time on one activity, the opportunity cost is the value of other activities that could have been pursued during that same time. If you spend your Monday afternoon playing video games, you cannot spend your Monday afternoon also playing hockey. The opportunity cost of playing video games is not being able to play hockey.

This concept reveals that the true cost of any choice extends beyond direct expense but also includes the value of the best alternative not chosen. People face opportunity costs when choosing time, money, or attention across competing priorities. For example, a student choosing to attend university full-time has not only direct costs like tuition and books but also the opportunity cost of potential income from full-time employment during those same years.

A decision to spend weekend hours working has the opportunity cost of leisure, family time, personal projects, or hobbies being lost. In a business, limited resources create opportunity costs when used in specific activity, department, or investment is chosen because they cannot be used in all of those.

Not recognizing opportunity costs often leads to their underestimation or neglect. Unlike direct costs that appear on financial statements, opportunity costs are invisible without deliberately considering them. This requires identifying all possible alternatives and estimating there potential value.

The concept of opportunity cost relates to economic principles critical to decision-making. By uncovering hidden costs, the concept of opportunity cost provides the foundation for solid economic analysis.

Price is the leading factor in how resources get used. People are constantly frustrated that they can't buy everything they want. A free-market economy is often called 'a profit system.' It is more accurate to call it a profit-and-loss system. Both profit and losses tell producers what to sell and what not to sell. To keep their business profitable producers constantly adjust to what customers want and can afford. They use scarce resources wisely making decisions based on prices and opportunity cost.

One commodity that is consistently high priced is waterfront property. Waterfront properties in Michigan that have the same size lot and similar house can be two, three or even ten times as much as property close by that is not on the water. That is because waterfront property is scarce and many desire to live there. Real property almost never goes down in value because no one is making any more land. Michigan has 12,000 lakes and all the frontage is owned by someone.

This brings us to another basic principle of economics, The **Law of Demand.** What the **Law of Demand** says is, as price goes down consumer demand goes up. Inversely, as prices increase consumer demand goes down.

Notice that the Law of Demand does not take into consideration other factors that may drive demand up or down, just price. The Law of Demand assumes all other factors remain constant.

The law of demand affects anyone who participates in the market as a buyer. It explains how people change their purchasing habits in response to changing prices.

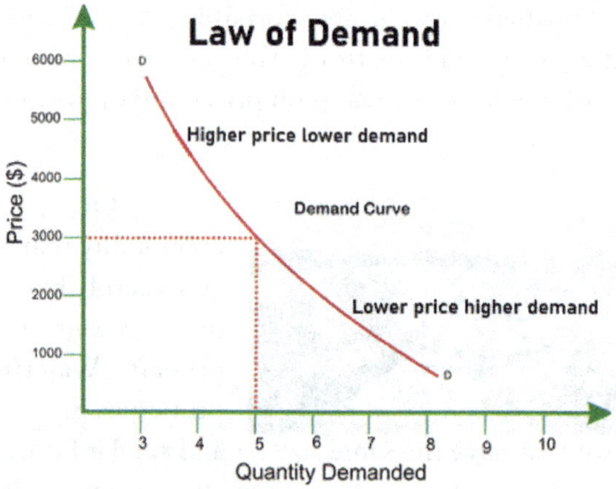

If you own a cell phone, you have probably experienced the law of demand with respect to monthly charges. When the monthly charge is low, people use the phone more. When the monthly charge goes up, people limit usage to an amount that holds the cost down.

The producer must ask, can I sell this product at a price that creates demand. The buyer asks, can I purchase this at a price I can afford. Any decision to buy is always accompanied by considering the opportunity cost.

Growing Money

For individuals, handling money comes down to a choice of what to do with money earned.

My uncle Jim said, **"Once I have some money, I will make it work for me, instead of me working for it."**

He invested in a business that repaired machines which produced enough money to buy Uncle Jim tailored suits and a Cadillac during the depression of the 1930s. During World War II he served in Great Britain where he began investing in racehorses. He retired to a posh estate in Surry, England where he lived until the 1990s. Uncle Jim learned very early the power of **investment**.

Borrowing money is a favorite American way to get the lifestyle they desire. This results in debt that may become unpayable at some point. It is better to invest and let the investment work for us. The worst that can happen is the loss of the investment, not your living standard. If that happens it is a lot less painful than debt.

There are a lot of things to invest in even in a weak **business climate.** The current business climate is one of good financial institutions, with low unemployment, steady sales, and stable national and foreign economic conditions.

The common choices for investment are stocks, bonds, real estate, direct lending, venture capital, art, jewels and precious metals. Guess which has the best chance of not losing its value and which has the highest risk.

Jewels, precious metals and real estate rarely lose value and are never worthless. Stocks give the highest **ROI,** return on investment, yet are at the highest risk with a potential to fall to no value.

Stocks are small shares of ownership in a company. People buy them to make money by trying to buy the stock share at low cost and sell it when it is high. Stocks also pay annual dividends to shareholders, called **dollars per share**, determined by the board of directors of the company. Companies want to pay dividends to shareholders so that investors will hold their stock and not sell it. When shareholders sell, the value of the stock can fall. The company wants people to keep stock because stock sales provide investment money for the company. If shareholders lose confidence in a company, they sell the stock, the value falls, more shares may be sold until the value falls to nothing, and the company folds.

When shareholder confidence is high, more stock is purchased, driving the price higher and the investment too. That is good for the company and good for the investor.

There are several **stock markets** in which one can invest. The NYSE New York Stock Exchange in New York City has been in business since the late 1700s. The NASDAQ is also in New York City. There are stock exchanges around the world like the London Stock Exchange in England, the Tokyo Stock Exchange in Japan and the Shenzhen Stock Exchange in communist China.

To make a buy, an investor uses a **broker. A broker handles buying and selling of investments.** There is always some kind of fee paid to the broker. A great deal of stock buying is done online these days. This has increased exchange activity around the world.

What happens when money is invested may happen as follows: Jim buys 100 shares of Flubadub Company stock that sells at $1.29 per share for $129.00 plus a 1% purchase fee from the broker. During the next month Flubadub sales soar and the stock goes up in value to $2.11 per share. Jim has almost doubled his investment. In the following six months Flubadub continues to rise in value to $5.18 per share, four times the original value. If Jim sells those shares now, he will be paid $518.00, minus the broker fees. Jim decides to hold on to his stock.

Perhaps a Flubadub competitor comes into the market in the next year selling the same product cheaper. In less than three months they drive Flubadub from the market, driving Flubadub stock to less than a dollar as shareholders sell their shares. The Flubadub shares drop to $.46 per share. Jim now has lost more than half his original investment. Jim must decide to hang on to the stock hoping it will go back up or sell and limit his loss.

He may decide to buy more shares at $.46. If he buys $100 worth of shares now, he will get more than 200 shares. If the stock recovers, he will be well ahead of his original investment with a good profit.

Bonds are a debt security, similar to an I.O.U. When you purchase a bond, you are lending money to a government, municipality, or corporation, known as an **issuer**. In return for that money, the issuer provides you with a promise to pay a specified rate of interest during the life of the bond and the face value of the bond when it **matures** or comes payable. The nature of a bond makes it more secure than stocks. With a bond, the promise to pay makes the return to the investor guaranteed. The amount the investor makes is less than may be made in the more-risky stock purchases.

Sample corporate bond

Venture capital is money invested in new companies just getting started that need money to get going. These are often new technology companies such as biotechnology, computers, or software, but they could be any business. The investor, called a venture capitalist, makes money usually by part-ownership in the company. This is a very risky investment causing the investor to want a high financial return on investment in a short, specified period of time.

Investing in gold for financial survival has become common as the entire world now is on a fiat monetary system. Gold has become a safe haven for many investors who fear that the creation of fiat dollars will not stop until the dollar is worthless. Gold has stood the test of time; paper money has not. The current price per ounce is $2,650.00.

Gold continues to be a universal currency and is held in reserve by the leading central banks. Central banks are becoming net buyers of gold.

Investing in silver is cheaper than gold with faster gains and losses. The current price is $80.00 per ounce. Silver has a high demand from the industrial sector guaranteeing price stability.

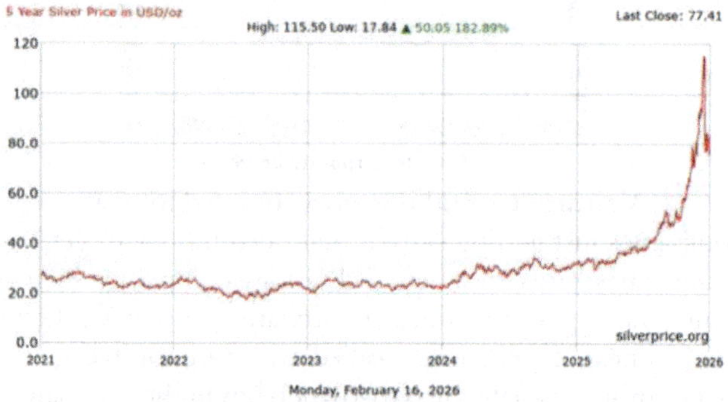

Compound interest, the secret every investor must know. What is compound interest?

Albert Einstein allegedly called compound interest "the eighth wonder of the world." Whether he said it or not, compound interest is genie of economics. Let's rub the lamp.

Interest is a payment an investor gets for loaning money. Compound interest is the earning of interest on both the money invested, called the principal, and the interest paid. Unlike simple interest, which is calculated only on the principal, compound interest makes the investment grow exponentially.

Think of a snowball rolling down a hill. The ball starts small, but as it rolls down the hill and collects more snow, it grows larger. When money is put into an investment, the account balance starts off small. Then as the interest is added to the account it begins to grow, and as more interest is added it grows faster and faster.

Let's look at an example with numbers. Fritz is 22 years old and just started her first job out of college. He starts an investment account and puts $1,000 in it right away. Each month, he adds $100 to the account and invests in an S&P 500 index fund. After 20 years, assuming the S&P 500 grows 7% a year on average, Fritz will have over $56,000 in his account! He will have paid $25,000 of his own money but has earned over $31,000 in compound interest! Compound interest now makes up most of the balance in Fritz's investment account. That's the power of compound interest.

To know how fast your investment money doubles use the **Rule of 72**. Just divide 72 by the interest rate.
For example:

At 1% interest, your money doubles in 72 years
72 divided by 1% = 72.
72 divided by 3% = 24 years
72 divided by 4% = 18 years
72 divided by 7% = 10.2 years
72 divided by 10% = 7.2 years
The higher the rate, the faster your money grows.

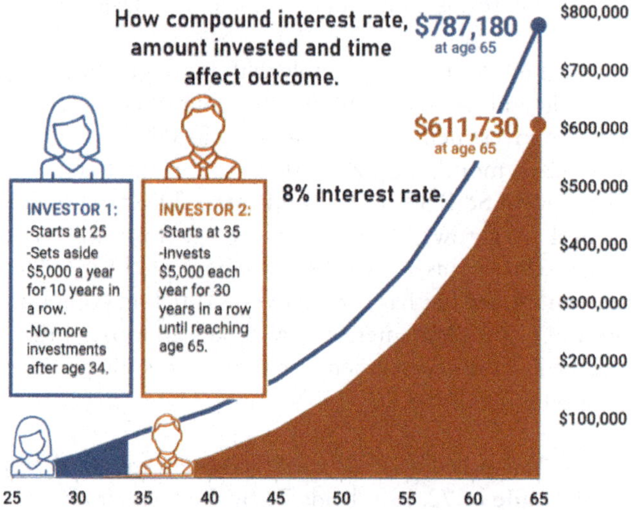

If those investment ideas don't get you, how about the following fact? Invested money value grows even while you sleep.

The SAP Factor

There is a wonderful and ever popular lie that if no money is used to get a service or a property it is free. All of us have benefited from provisions we did not pay for with money or favor. People like to say that air is free. You don't have to pay to breathe. Certainly, no one charges you to breathe, except under a respirator in a hospital. God gave you lungs free, legs free, your whole self for free. Only, don't tell that to your mother who carried you around for months, then worked like a weightlifter for endless hours to bring you into the world. Also, remember that your body works so you can breathe. No, you don't have to think about it yet work goes on.

There is a place online called, "Totally Free Stuff." You can get amazing things there; peanut butter, magazines, software, baseball tickets, medical samples, and that's not all. Do you really believe that these things are completely free? Each item cost someone something.

Consider what most of us get for free in everyday life, lunch, tickets, rides, and even books. Still, those things did not come into existence on their own. Someone worked to make them. God worked for six days to create the world we enjoy. He rested on the seventh day. If things aren't free for God, they are not going to be free for you.

The truth is the
SAP factor rules all of life.
The SAP factor says:
SOMEONE ALWAYS PAYS.

What might be free for you will cost someone either work or money. The SAP factor is unavoidable, and nobody wants to be a sap.

Economics is the exchange of work, property, and money. The rest is theory and complicated made-up names and concepts. Like music, economics can be played in an unknown number of ways. The objective of this book is to make it simple. **Nothing is free**.

Advertisers offer free stuff to get people to become customers. Either they give a free thing to get people to buy more, or to make them a potential customer, or to get them to buy some other product they make. The old "free sample" is offered often because it gets people to buy the product when the sample runs out.

It might be assumed that the company pays for the "free sample".

BEEP! Wrong!

Hard as it is to believe companies don't pay for anything. **WHAT!** Companies that pay out too much money quickly go broke. Only companies that make money stay in business. Think, if a company is going to sell something all their cost, for everything, must be covered by the sale. Everything includes buildings, equipment, labor, material, power, taxes and FREE SAMPLES. Who pays? The customers pay. They pay for everything when they buy products or services. Sales to customers are the only source of income for any business. It is not mean, or a trick, or unfair, it is the **SAP factor.**

Does that mean that the SAP factor is an economic fact? OH YEAH, you're catchin' on!

The author denies that the name "SAP factor" can be found in any other book on economics, money or other financial study, but it exists nonetheless:

SOMEBODY ALWAYS PAYS!

This brings us to the issue of who pays corporate taxes: "corporation" being another term for any business. Since customers pay for everything, or the corporation goes broke, it means the customers pay the corporate taxes. Once again, it is not sleight of hand, it is the SAP factor.

To make any business survive it must make money. Money is not made by giving things away. When business costs go up the customer must pay more. When the government raises business taxes, the customer pays the increase, not the business.

"That's not fair", Screams my Auntie Kaplis, who is head of the Even Distribution Society. "Those dollars should come from their evil corporate profits."

Dear old Auntie Kaplis doesn't want anyone to take advantage of customers. She is always watching out for the little guy. She knows those profits come from the customers, and she believes that increased costs should be taken from profits.

To understand what she wants, profit must be understood. **Profit is the amount of money left after a business pays all its expenses.** Usually that is summed up at the end of a fiscal year. A fiscal year may not end on December 31st, it is often a year related to the date bookkeeping began. Profit is a measure of the fiscal wellbeing of a business. Companies that don't make a good profit are likely to fail.

What happens to that profit money depends on the type of company. Most businesses are for profit operations.

Types of businesses:

First, the **private business** is owned by one or a few people, the profit is the owner's, they may do as they please with it. The private company gets to keep profit and transfer as much as they like into their personal bank accounts after they pay tax on it. **It is from profit that government takes taxes.**

What keeps companies from taking an unfair amount from their customers is competition. If one business raises prices too high, another will tend to take away business with a lower price. New companies are always coming to the market with lower prices, better services, and products. **Competition drives the market.** The more successful a company is the more likely it is to be the target of its competition.

Small profits put a business at severe risk if sudden economic conditions cause a downturn. Profits represent a buffer against poor sales.

A business cannot afford to let profits sit around since they will be taxed. A business will spend or invest as much profit as possible, which benefits other businesses. Profit earned each year represents the measure of business success. **The entire reason for risking a fortune in a business is to make a profit**.

Second, the **public business** is owned by the stockholders who will expect a share of the profits, called a dividend. The more profit, the higher the dividend for stockholders. Public companies must answer their stockholders. Want to own a big company? Buy their stock. Even one share makes you a stockholder, an owner, with a vote at their annual meeting. Investors wanting to be stockholders look for companies with strong profits.

Stock sales provide investment money for a public company's operation. When profits of a public company decline, stockholders lose interest and sell their stock. Selling off a company's stock reduces the stock value and the funds available to run that company. The company must improve sales by making a good profit by selling stocks to get more investment money. Investors constantly watch the stock markets, investing in stocks as stock values go up and sell stock when stock prices go down. For public companies, profit is not a luxury. **Profits are the single most significant factor in their financial condition and survival.** A public company without profit will go bankrupt.

Third, the **not-for-profit business** has a board of directors who can do whatever they please with money not spent on annual expenses. They remain tax free under Internal Revenue Service code 501(c).

One year Blue-Cross, a non-profit, spent one million dollars on a large rectangular sculpture for their offices in Detroit. It is sometimes thought that there is something philanthropic about non-profit. The truth is it takes three people to start a non-profit.

The only difference between a non-profit and a profit business is how they report earnings. The non-profit company does not report the funds left after all expenses are paid, they neither report profit, nor pay tax on it.

The public company, the one with stockholders, must report their earnings both to the government and to the stockholders. If they do not report a profit to the stockholders, the stocks may begin to be sold at a rapid rate, putting the company in danger of failure. Non-profit companies do not report to stockholders or pay taxes.

All business types must compete. **Competition levels of the playing field in business.** Even a non-profit cannot afford to lose money for long.

Profits are only seen as "evil" by people, like my Auntie Kaplis, who do not own a business. That is because people who do not own a business do not understand **risk.**

Risk is the constant possibility of monetary loss. Anyone in America can start a business; yes, even you. You do not need money to start a business. You do not need a building to start a business. You do not need equipment to start a business. What you need is a lot of guts. A person going into business must be willing to take risks from the moment the business starts, and as long as it lasts. There is never a time when a business is not at risk. The types of risk are many.

The Small Business Association claims more than half of all businesses will fail in the first five years. Here's their reasons why:

1. Lack of experience
2. Insufficient capital: meaning money
3. Poor location
4. Poor inventory management
5. Over-investment in equipment
6. Poor credit arrangements
7. Personal use of business funds
8. Unexpected growth
9. Competition
10. Low sales

Small companies aren't the only ones to fail. Big companies such as automobile companies fail too. Since

World War II twenty-five automobile manufacturers have gone broke in America.

Included in the list are Packard, Willis, Kaiser, Delorean, Hudson, Nash, American Motors, Studebaker, Franklin, and let's not forget General Motors.

General Motors, in the 1970s, was the largest company in the world. GM sneered at foreign makers who challenged their position. Their ability to compete failed when their size and poor business practices resulted in such a loss of profits it forced them into bankruptcy in 2009.

Other major companies have failed too. That list includes **Enron** once valued at $90 billion and the 7th largest company in the United States, went bankrupt because of foolish speculation by overzealous managers.

Washington Mutual, the sixth largest bank in the U.S. After a 10-day run on the bank with total withdrawals of more than $16 billion, the US government seized Washington Mutual's assets.

Bethlehem Steel built the first blast furnace. They made steel for railroads, skyscrapers, coal, nuclear reactors, warships, cargo vessels, and large construction projects. Cheap imports led to bankruptcy in 2001.

Pan Am Airlines, founded in 1927, an airline that was part of American culture for most of the 20th century. Unfortunately, Federal deregulation and new competition caused the airline to collapse in 1991.

The **Commodore Computer 64** had about 50% of the personal computer market and scared the pants off Apple, Atari and other pc makers of the 1980s. The company went bankrupt in the spring of 1994.

In all business failures, the SAP factor causes the unpaid bills of these companies to be absorbed by the creditors that were owed money. Those creditors make up for the loss with higher prices to their customers. It is harder for customers to detect when there are losses because the money trail goes through courts taking time. In the end, the SAP factor rules. Even in **bankruptcy** the customer pays.

Notice how the SAP factor always leads back to the same payers. The people who buy products and services pay all the expenses. They pay off bankruptcy, theft, embezzlement, and any other business losses. There is no escape from the SAP factor. Customers either pay the business, or in the event of bankruptcy, the creditors, who get their money from their customers.

People like my Auntie Kaplis never think about the risk every business must face, or the fact that profit is essential to staying in business. Company owners run such risks to make a profit. Without profit the business dies.

The SAP factor cannot be avoided in the exchange of goods and services.

The Father of Economics

Adam Smith

In the 18th century, England practiced **mercantilism**. This economic system attempted to increase the nation's wealth by imposing strong government regulation on all commercial activity. England forced the American colonies to do business only with England and no other country. Mercantilism proposed that national strength increases by limiting imports through tariffs and maximizing exports.

Adam Smith, a Scottish philosopher, argued against this system. Smith believed such a system could not be maintained forever, because the global economy would become stagnant if every country wanted to export, and no one wanted to import. He too denied the idea that the wealth of a nation depended primarily on the possession of precious metals. His thinking, and his famous published work, *The Wealth of Nations*, caused him to become known as the "father of economics." Not all his ideas were original, though no one had put them together in a single philosophical work until Smith did it.

Unfortunately, it set economics in a separate sphere in which it might be studied as if it had nothing to do with the rest of life. This is a favorite game of intellectuals, to set subjects in individual boxes causing students to forget its ties to the other subjects that have been put in other boxes. It is a dire mistake to try to separate economics from the rest of life; ask anyone who runs a business, a household, or holds a government office.

The Wealth of Nations helped to move industry from home-based operations to wealth created by assembly-line production through a division of labor. Smith showed that one man working alone took 18 steps required to make a sewing pin. One man could make only a handful of pins each week. If the 18 steps were completed in an assembly-line fashion by 10 men, each repeatedly performing only one or two functions, production would jump to thousands of pins per week. Thousands more than all ten men could produce working individually.

His **Laissez-faire** philosophy taught limiting government intervention and taxation in the marketplace. He developed the idea of the "**invisible hand**" behind **supply** and **demand**. As seen in the following quote:

> *"Every individual necessarily labors to render the annual revenue of the society as great as he can. He generally neither intends to promote the public interest, nor knows how much he is promoting it ... He intends only his own gain, and he is in this, as in many other cases, led by an invisible hand to promote an end which was no part of his intention. Nor is it always the worse for society that it was no part of his intention. By pursuing his own interest he frequently promotes*

that of the society more effectually than when he really intends to promote it. I have never known much good done by those who affected to trade for the public good."

These ideas point to what some call the **Smith Dictum** that each person in seeking their own self-interest results in the best for everyone.

"It is not from the benevolence of the butcher, the brewer, or the baker, that we can expect our dinner, but from their regard to their own interest,"
Adam Smith

By selling products that people want to buy, sellers hope to make money. If they meet the needs of their customers, they will make a meaningful income. By running their business for the sole purpose of earning money, they are providing products and services that customers want. Such a system, Smith argued, creates wealth not just for the business owner, it extends to the entire nation increasing the wealth and well-being of the

country. Smith established the concept that a man who invests his wealth in his business will help himself earn the highest return. That high return benefits both the government and the general wealth of the nation.
Adam Smith's ideas became the foundation of the **classical school of economics**. His principles have outlasted many other complex economic concepts that followed. His ideas served as the basis for further explorations in economics, both for and against his precepts. Smith died in 1790, but the ideas he promoted live on live on. In 2007, the Bank of England placed his image on the twenty-pound note.

The Parable of the Broken Window

Frequently in economics it is easy to see one cost or benefit while not detecting hidden ones. This is demonstrated in a parable proposed by **Frederic Bastiat** in 1850 essay *Ce qu'on voit et ce qu'on ne voit pas*, or *That Which is Seen and That Which is not Seen.* The parable demonstrates the economic principles of **opportunity costs** and the "**law of unintended consequences**." Familiarity with this parable provides a significant building block for the study of economics.

The parable:

> *"Have you ever witnessed the anger of the good shopkeeper, James Goodfellow, when his careless son happened to break a pane of glass? If you have been present at such a scene, you will most assuredly bear witness to the fact that every one of the spectators, were there even thirty of them, by common consent apparently, offered the unfortunate owner this invariable consolation—"It is an ill wind that blows nobody good. Everybody must live, and what would become of the glaziers if panes of glass were never broken?"*

Now, this form of condolence contains an entire theory, which it will be well to show up in this simple case, seeing that it is precisely the same as that which, unhappily, regulates the greater part of our economical institutions.

Suppose it cost six francs to repair the damage, and you say that the accident brings six francs to the glazier's trade—that it encourages that trade to the amount of six francs—I grant it; I have not a word to say against it; you reason justly. The glazier comes, performs his task, receives his six francs, rubs his hands, and, in his heart, blesses the careless child. All this is that which is seen.

But if, on the other hand, you come to the conclusion, as is too often the case, that it is a good thing to break windows, that it causes money to circulate, and that the encouragement of industry in general will be the result of it, you will oblige me to call out, "Stop there! Your theory is confined to that which is seen; it takes no account of that which is not seen."

It is not seen that as our shopkeeper has spent six francs upon one thing, he cannot spend them upon another. It is not seen that if he had not had a window to replace, he would, perhaps, have replaced his old shoes, or added another book to his library. In short, he would have employed his six francs in some way, which this accident has prevented."

It may also be said that this needed window will have a positive effect on the glazier. This depends on the glazier's availability of time and resource. If the glazier has other situations demanding his time and supplies, the conflict may cause him a loss. In this case, the broken window makes the glazier and the shopkeeper poorer by the value of the window. Otherwise, one might decide to smash all the windows in town in the name of creating prosperity. Certainly, one would not suggest destroying the town creates prosperity.

All of this is to show why destruction, great or small, is not a benefit to the society as a whole. It also shows that to make good economic judgments one must look at all the possible factors involved.

To gain understanding without missing all the information economists use **macroeconomics**, the study of the economy as a whole. This is different from **microeconomics**, which studies individuals and how they make economic decisions. Economists using macroeconomics analyze various economic indicators that tell the relative health of an economy. They analyze the macro economy by primarily looking at national output, unemployment, inflation, and consumers who ultimately determine the direction of an economy.

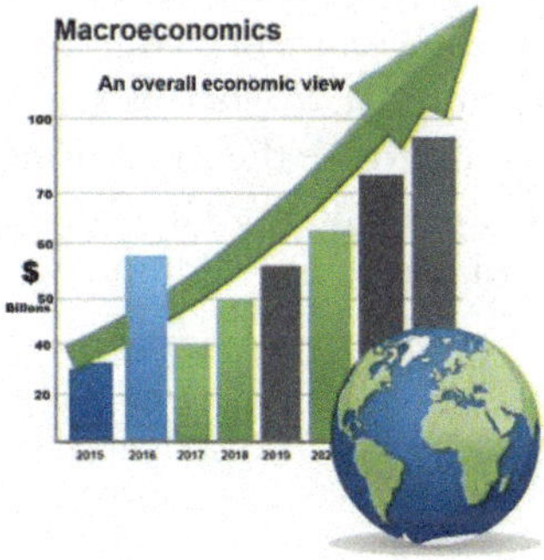

Macroeconomics began with a significant publication by John Maynard Keynes's, *General Theory of Employment, Interest, and Money*. When the Great Depression struck, classical economists had difficulty explaining how an economy could become stagnant. In classical theory, prices and wages drop until all goods and labor are attractive to buy. Then demand brings the market back. Keynes offered a new theory of economics that explained why markets might not recover. In Keynes's theory, people and businesses tend to hold on to their cash in tough economic times. Keynes explained how panic driven economic behavior would magnify a small decrease in consumption or investment and cause declines throughout the economy. Keynes also noted the role uncertainty can play in the economy.

By the 1950s, most economists had accepted this view of the macro economy. Economists like Paul Samuelson, Franco Mondigliani, James Tobin, and Robert Solow developed formal **Keynesian models**, and contributed formal theories of consumption, investment, and money demand that filled out the Keynesian framework.

The truth is Keynes changed his mind so many times about the operation of the economy it is unfair to stick him with any one theory. The one theory he cannot escape is that of encouraging the government to dump money into the economy to stimulate it. Politicians starting with Franklin Roosevelt latched on to the theory of using government funds to stimulate the economy. The fact that the practice always fails does not discourage additional government expenditures.

In opposition to Keynesian economics stands the **Austrian theory** of the business cycles. Austrian economists focus on the credit cycle as the primary cause of most business cycles. Austrian economists assert that damaging and ineffective central bank policies are the cause of most business cycles. Central banks err by setting artificial interest rates, resulting in excessive credit creation, speculative "bubbles" and artificially low savings.

Friedrich Hayek was one of the few economists who gave warning about a major economic crisis before the great crash of 1929. In February 1929, Hayek warned that the coming financial crisis was an unavoidable consequence of reckless monetary expansion. Note that he did not warn of the Great Depression that would follow, no one predicted that event.

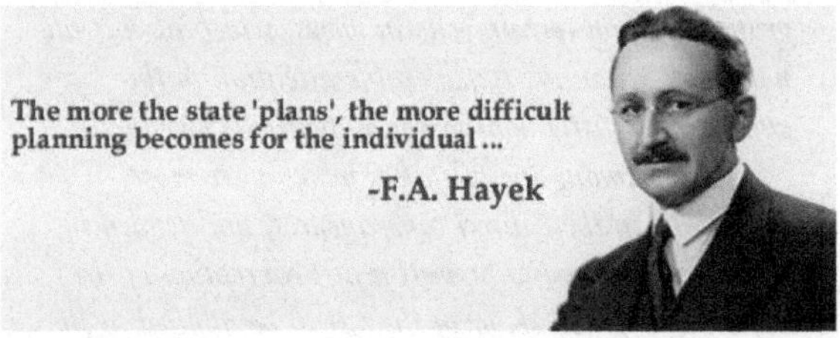

Hayek was an economist and philosopher best known for his defense of classical liberalism and free market capitalism against socialist and collectivist thought. He is considered to be one of the most important economists and political philosophers of the twentieth century, winning the Nobel Memorial Prize in Economic Sciences in 1974.

In his essay, *The Use of Knowledge in Society*, he argued that a central bank neither possesses the relevant information which should govern the supply of money, nor does it have the ability to use that information correctly. This is the fulfilment of the *Parable of the Broken*

Window. The core issue of the parable is complete knowledge of economic situations in which every unintended consequence is discovered.

The idea of government taxing and spending to create prosperity is older than Keynes. **John Stuart Mill** wrote an attack on the idea in 1844. The following are his opening remarks:

"Before the appearance of those great writers whose discoveries have given to political economy its present comparatively scientific character, the ideas universally entertained both by theorists and by practical men, on the causes of national wealth, were grounded upon certain general views, which almost all who have given any considerable attention to the subject now justly hold to be completely erroneous.

Among the mistakes which were most pernicious in their direct consequences, and tended in the greatest degree to prevent a just conception of the objects of the science, or of the test to be applied to the solution of the questions which it presents, was the immense importance attached to consumption. The great end of legislation in matters of national wealth, according to the prevalent opinion, was to create consumers. A great and rapid consumption was what the producers, of all classes and denominations, wanted, to enrich themselves and the country. This object, under the varying names of an extensive demand, a brisk circulation, a great expenditure of money, and sometimes totidem verbis a large consumption, was conceived to be the great condition of prosperity.

It is not necessary, in the present state of the science, to contest this doctrine in the most flagrantly absurd of its forms or of its applications. The utility of a large government expenditure, for the purpose of encouraging industry, is no longer maintained. Taxes are not now esteemed to be "like the dews of heaven, which return again in prolific showers." It is no longer supposed that you benefit the producer by taking his money, provided you give it to him again in exchange for his goods. There is nothing which impresses a person of reflection with a stronger sense of the shallowness of the political reasoning of the last two centuries, than the general reception so long given to a doctrine which, if it proves anything, proves that the more you take from the pockets of the people to spend on your own pleasures, the richer they grow; that the man who steals money out of a shop, provided he expends it all again at the same shop, is a benefactor to the tradesman whom he robs, and that the same operation, repeated sufficiently often, would make the tradesman's fortune.

In opposition to these palpable absurdities, it was triumphantly established by political economists, that consumption never needs encouragement. All which is produced is already consumed, either for the purpose of reproduction or of enjoyment. The person who saves his income is no less a consumer than he who spends it: he consumes it in a different way; it supplies food and clothing to be consumed, tools and materials to be used, by productive laborers. Consumption, therefore, already takes place to the greatest extent which the amount of production admits of; but, of the two kinds of consumption, reproductive and unproductive, the former alone adds to the national wealth, the latter impairs it. What is consumed for mere enjoyment, is gone; what is consumed for reproduction, leaves commodities of equal value, commonly with the addition of a profit. The usual effect of the attempts of government to encourage consumption, is merely to prevent saving; that is, to promote unproductive consumption at the expense of reproductive, and diminish the national wealth by the very means which were intended to increase it.

What a country wants to make it richer, is never consumption, but production."

Mill's commentary refutes, among other false ideas, the idea of the helpful loss in *Parable of the Broken Window.*

Capitalism

"Capitalism is not an 'ism.' It is closer to being the opposite of an 'ism,' because it is simply the freedom of ordinary people to make whatever economic transactions they can mutually agree to."

Thomas Sowell

The word capitalism is often misused and poorly understood. The presumption about its meaning varies depending on who and why it is being used. Let's break down the word from a linguistic stance first.

It comes from Latin *capitalis* meaning 'the head of,' from the Latin *caput* meaning 'head.' The "ism" part of capitalism is a suffix that tells us the noun prefix is a practice, system or doctrine. Ism comes from Latin *isma* signifying to 'practice or teach something.'

Among other meanings the noun **capital** is now defined as wealth in the form of money or property owned by a person or business and human resources of economic value. One would assume that capitalism then is a practice, system or doctrine having to do with wealth in the form of property or money owned by a person.

Since it is often referred to as an economic system. One might assume, from the way the word capitalism is used, that someone, or some group, conceived this practice or system and put it out as an intellectual idea. Socialism was first put forth by Plato. Communism was put forth by Marx. Who was it that put forth capitalism? The answer is no one. It has always been practiced, but it is neither a system nor a doctrine. It is human behavior. It is just something people do. There is no theory, there is no doctrine of capitalism.

Capitalism began the first time a poor ancient fellow noticed his friend had made a superior spear. Seeing the object and wanting one he approaches the friend asking how he made it. Finding the difficulty of making such a device is too hard to do on a first try, he asks the neighbor what he might do to get him to make such a spear for him. The neighbor agrees to make the spear if he would exchange it for one of his clever fishnets he makes. **They exchange goods and services in which both perceive to have gained something.** That is the core of capitalism.

Today business is more complex than our ancient neighbors, but the behavior is the same. The aim of capitalism is to gain from an exchange which is often the motive to make a profit. As Adam Smith, the father of modern economics, said:

"It is not from the benevolence of the butcher, the brewer, or the baker that we expect our dinner, but from their regard to their own interest."

Both parties to any voluntary exchange of goods or services have their own interest in the outcome, both must believe they have gained.

Capitalism is only possible if people are free to own and exchange without any outside interference.

First is the freedom to own private property, such as tangible assets: land, equipment and buildings; or intangible assets: such as stocks and bonds.

Second is the freedom of self-interest, in which people make exchanges without regard for outside interference.

Third is freedom to set prices and enter competition.

All this requires a limited role of government, to protect the rights of private citizens and facilitate proper functioning of markets.

A capitalist economy is often also called a **market economy** because market economy implies that the market not some outside authority controls the economy. A market being the place in which goods and services are exchanged.

Pure capitalism is a **free-market** or **laissez-faire** market. Laissez-faire is French for 'let it be' or leave it alone. In it, individuals may determine where to invest, what to produce or sell, and at what prices to exchange goods and services. The laissez-faire marketplace operates without checks or controls.

Today, most countries practice a mixed capitalist system that includes some degree of government regulation of business and some extent of public ownership of certain industries.

Good ol' Auntie Kaplis likes to complain that capitalism is just selfish.

"They just do it for the money. They don't give a hoot for the little guy. They make products or services and won't give them to the people that really need them. They don't care about anyone; they only want what's in it for themselves. They are just greedy."

She is right; people do go into business to make money for themselves. They sell to those who can afford their products or services. She is also right that their interest is in themselves; it is self-interest that drives them. She is wrong in implying that self-interest is bad, or that it is greed. Self-interest is the virtue that makes business work.

"You rascal!" She calls out, "how can self-interest be a virtue?"

Take a simple example from life, Charlie Barnes likes to plow the soil and grow food. Sam Husbandman likes to raise chickens, pigs and cows. Other people around the town are teachers, lawyers, police officers, firefighters, store owners, laborers, and whatever. They depend on Charlie and Sam to sell to the grocer so they can have food. Charlie and Sam know if their product isn't good, or someone else produces it for less, they are out of business. The grocer knows he must sell the packaged food at an acceptable price, and he must have it ready when the customers want it.

Charlie and Sam and the grocer are in business only as long as they please others. They want to stay in business to provide for their own families. Their livelihood comes from their business. The more successful their business the better their lives will be; that is self-interest. Knowing how to feed that self-interest is the trick. If they do not serve the interest of others their interest is not served either.

Consider the golden rule: "Do unto others as you would have them do unto you." It is God's rule which holds for economics too. Is the golden rule a virtue?

Jesus also warned, "Love your neighbor as you love yourself." He understands that men love themselves. He wants us to understand how to use that measure of love to handle others.

The self-interest of the business owner becomes a virtue making him care for those around him. By caring for them he takes care of himself and his household.

Communism & Socialism

"Socialism in general has a record of failure so blatant that only an intellectual could ignore or evade it."
Thomas Sowell

Communism and Socialism are economic theories put forward by famous men. Plato proposed **communism** in his dialogue *The Republic*. He was seeking the perfect form of government. What he liked best was a government run by Philosopher-Kings. Being a philosopher, Plato thought they were the best possible type of people to run government.

These Philosopher-Kings would make sure all goods and services were evenly distributed to all people. That no one would be poor, hungry, not taken care of well. The Philosopher Kings would be of such virtuous character that they would do nothing wrong.

Sounds good. Plato did not explain where one would find people of the character needed to be a Philosopher King.

This is the fatal flaw of communism or socialism. That feeding one's own interest does not go away when one is a communist. It is human behavior.

Socialism is supposed to be different from **communism** according to some intellectuals. The definitions contradict that idea. They are both defined as: **a political economic system in which the government owns and distributes the means of producing goods and services.**

The real difference between communism and socialism is spelling.

The communist Soviet Union from 1918 until 1990 called itself **The Union of Soviet Socialist Republics.**

A socialist friend claims that in his socialist country the government makes sure everyone is provided for no matter what their income. One need not worry about health care, college, old age, unemployment, or any other problem no matter how little money they make.

In his country doctors and hospitals are in short supply, as they are in socialist Canada and Great Britain, Cuba and Venezuela. People living there often go to the United States, Turkey, or Hungary for medical care to avoid a long wait for surgery or other treatment. Socialist governments keep healthcare costs low by limiting the amount available. Why should those hospital administrators and doctors care how long a patient waits for care? In socialist countries, they will not lose their job no matter what happens to the patient, or how they complain.

Under socialism the worker has a guaranteed job and a guaranteed income. Nothing motivates him to provide good service, product, or convenience to his customers.

In the ideal socialist regimes of the Soviet Union and Cuba there was no shopping. Long lines formed at the few poorly supplied stores where people had a chance, maybe, to get necessities. If there was no meat, too bad, come back next week, maybe there will be some. Store managers didn't care. Neither did the people supplying the stores.

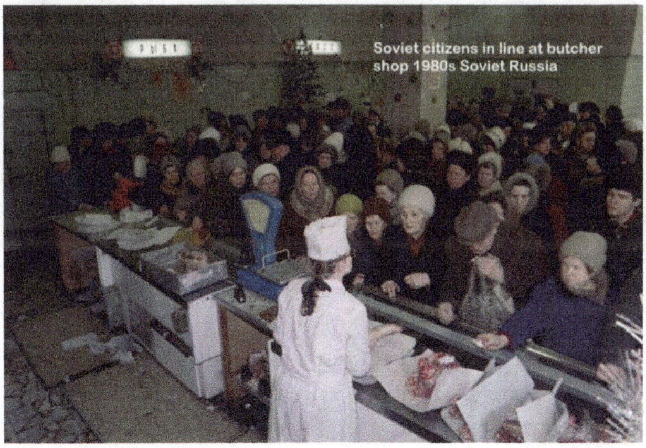

Communists claim a utopian society in which no one pays for anything. It is the concept expressed by Karl Marx in his 1948 Communist Manifesto: **"From each according to his ability to each according to his need"**.

Chrysler engineers were shocked by the comments of a Russian Jew who escaped from the old Soviet Union to come to work at Chrysler in the 1980s. He told of the horrible conditions in the engineering office where he worked in Soviet Russia. Engineers came in drunk in the morning. They slept at their desk and could not be fired from their state guaranteed position. The lack of motivation to complete projects was universal. No one cared because they had nothing to gain from good performance. In the entire country, there was no self-interest to spur performance. No one asked the question, "What's in it for me?" In 1991 the Soviet Union collapsed because it went financially broke.

Socialist programs in basically capitalist countries also cause people not to care. Take unemployment payments. Workers do not care to go back to work when the government pays for them to stay home. This causes consistently high unemployment rates. The self-interest of the unemployed is fulfilled by the provision of a payment for doing nothing. It is harder to look for work when money is provided for no work. The attitude is perfectly expressed in the common response to the question of when one will return to work.

"I don't know, and I don't care."

College and retirement in socialist countries create lackadaisical monsters too. Since the state pays the way, the longest possible duration in these conditions is desirable. This results in great expense to the government. People in some socialist countries in Europe retire at 55 years of age on handsome pensions. These countries are finding it hard to pay these pensions as more people retire each year.

Under socialism the SAP factor still reigns supreme. What eventually happens when taxes can no longer cover promised social programs is the society collapses.

It is the collapse of the financial institutions that bring on the fall. This is precisely what has happened in Greece, Italy and Spain in recent times. It is a cataclysmic event. There was rioting in the street by people promised money and benefits the governments could no longer provide. The SAP factor will require someone to pay the bill for the socialist lack of self-interest.

These Greeks are destroying their own society which can no longer afford to pay them the excessive benefits once promised.
This is people replacing self-interest with greed.

As the industrial revolution expanded during the 18th and 19th century, critics expounded on the unhappy effects it had on the growing workforces gathering in factories. No previous model had existed to show how to make a safe, wholesome factory; there had never been such places before in history. The work proceeded as it had when done in the home or farm, with long hours, done by men, women and children of all ages.

The steam engine made the industrial revolution possible. It provided immense power needed to run factories and made it possible to build a factory anywhere. The steam engine to which long belts were attached drove the machinery. These contraptions crisscrossed the factory with no protection for the people working in them.

Material from operations filled the air so thick that dust explosions occurred all too often. In textile mills tiny fluffs of cotton floated like white mist. Factories were dirty, crowded, hazardous places to work. This is well documented by writers of the time such as Charles Dickens.

Workers had become as dependent on these factories for livelihood as they were miserable from working in them. Attempting to get better conditions and pay they grouped together to apply pressure on owners. This met with mild success and frequent abuse. Violence often erupted from these confrontations of union and management.

In the smoky shadow of these struggles an idea as old as philosophy yet new as industry emerged: **socialism**. Its appeal came from the concept of sharing wealth equally, a basic socialist principle.

A now notorious utopian of this movement, Karl Marx, became a critic of the worker management struggle of the industrial revolution. He and his friend Friedrich Engels wrote a short, incendiary work called the *Communist Manifesto*. Their aim went beyond settling the issues between workers and owners, to a revolution in which the workers would take control of all production, laws, courts, farms, family, religion, and property. The wealthy class would be forever wiped out from society. It is ironic that they wrote this manifesto while living on the money of Engels parents, who were rich industrialists.

According to the *Communist Manifesto,* all history boiled down to nothing more than the struggle between the rich, who Marx called "Bourgeoisie," and the workers, whom he called the "Proletariat." This simplistic view of history has and continues to have many followers. Appreciation of the *Communist Manifesto* persists despite its inability to explain the rise and fall of empires, the revelations of science, the cause of wars, the motivation for exploration, the nature of philosophy and education, or even the growth and constant changes of industry and business.

The tone of what the communists want is set early in the manifesto:

> *"The immediate aim of the Communists is the same as that of all other proletarian parties: Formation of the proletariat into a class, overthrow of the bourgeois supremacy, conquest of political power by the proletariat."*

This is quickly followed by thoughts on the central feature of communism:

In this sense, the theory of the Communists may be summed up in the single sentence: Abolition of private property."

His position ignores the fact that the more people who own property, the greater their prosperity is. During this industrial revolution property ownership grew more than in the rest of human history.

Here is Marx ten-point recitation on how everything is regulated in a communist society.

"*1. Abolition of property in land and application of all rents of land to public purposes.*

2. A heavy progressive or graduated income tax.

3. Abolition of all rights of inheritance.

4. Confiscation of the property of all emigrants and rebels.

5. Centralization of credit in the banks of the state, by means of a national bank with state capital and an exclusive monopoly.

6. Centralization of the means of communication and transport in the hands of the state.

7. Extension of factories and instruments of production owned by the state;

the bringing into cultivation of waste lands, and the improvement of the soil generally in accordance with a common plan.

8. Equal obligation of all to work. Establishment of industrial armies, especially for agriculture.

9. Combination of agriculture with manufacturing industries; gradual abolition of all the distinction between town and country by a more equable distribution of the populace over the country.

10. Free education for all children in public schools. Abolition of children's factory labor in its present form. Combination of education with industrial production, etc."

In all of this he gives no explanation as to how the economics will be implemented. He gives no reason why the economy will function, or what will drive it when the profit incentive is removed.

This ideology enjoyed appeal in most of the western world since it was published in 1848. Western governments struggled to prevent these concepts from becoming law with mixed success. In America, socialist and communist ideas and organizations have flourished since the 19th century. Their maxims gain the most popularity among intellectuals, educators, and the political elite. The progressive movement of the late 18th and early 19th century adhered to many communist precepts.

In Europe, socialism gained momentum in the early 19th century, becoming a credible threat to government and business in France, Germany, Italy and Spain.

Germany, determined to end the fighting on the Eastern front in World War I, sent the communist zealot Nicoli Lenin from a German prison to Russia. They intended for him to disrupt the country with a communist radical movement that would take Russia out of the war. The irony is that he started a revolution that ended with the formation of the Soviet Union.

It is also ironic that war, not the economic failure of capitalism, established the first great communist empire, the Soviet Union. After operating for seventy years the Soviet Union collapsed in 1991 because of its catastrophic economic failure. Communism and socialism always fail because the principles of economics are not followed.

Lenin giving a speech in Moscow

Communist philosophers came to America in the 1930s to escape Hitler's rise to power, and threat to their existence. They came to America not to enjoy freedom, but to destroy it. They believed that Marx's prediction of workers takeover had been prevented by people being blinded by capitalism. Their idea was to destroy our culture.

The group called the **Frankfort School** moved into American higher education at Columbia University. Theodor Adorno co-authored, *The Authoritarian Personality*. It redefined traditional American views on gender roles and sexual morals as "prejudice." Adorno compared them to the traditions that led to the rise of fascism in Europe.

It is no coincidence that the slur for the political right today is "fascist". Anyone holding to traditional values is called a fascist to crush their ideas without making an argument.

The Frankfort School moved its criticism away from economics and toward Freud by publishing works on psychological repression. Like Marx they split society into two main groups: the oppressors and the victims. They argued that history and reality were shaped by those who controlled traditional institutions. Next, they argued that the social roles of men and women were due to gender differences defined by the "oppressors." In other words, gender did not exist, it was merely a "social construct."

The social movements of the 1960s; black power, feminism, gay rights, sexual liberation, provided a unique vehicle to release cultural Marxist ideas into the mainstream. Railing against all things "establishment," The Frankfurt School's ideals caught on like wildfire across American universities. They continue to influence universities, entertainment, and the press to this day.

Communist China enters the free market:

Mao Tse Tong led a successful communist revolution in China after World War II. His economic programs led to mass starvation of about 20 million Chinese. His agrarian society failed repeatedly. Only after Mao's death did China moderate their rule of private ownership and began to become a world economic force.

Modern Hong Kong

When they took the city of Hong Kong back from the British, they were wise enough to allow free trade.

Hong Kong Stock Exchange

Hong Kong markets became the freest and most successful in the world.

Because of capitalist behavior in communist China, the city of Shanghai which had stagnated under communism since the 1930s became a thriving metropolis. This is shown in the Pudong District, which became a pilot area for private ownership. By the end of 2009, there were 787 financial institutions, of which 170 were owned

by foreign investors.

Shanghai Stock Exchange is the world's 5th largest stock market at $3.5 trillion as of February 2016, and 2nd largest in East Asia and Asia. Unlike the Hong Kong Stock Exchange, the Shanghai Stock Exchange is still not entirely open to foreign investors due to tight capital account controls exercised by the Chinese government and often manipulated by the decisions of the Chinese Communist party.

In the past two decades Shanghai has been one of the fastest growing cities in the world. All the Chinese had to do was abandon Marxist communism.

Even communists succeed when they embrace free markets.

Taxes, Inflation, and Debt, Oh My!

Albert Einstein said, "The hardest thing in the world to understand is the income tax." Albert was a genius. If he couldn't understand it, what chance do we have?

At the beginning of the United States there was no income tax. The founding fathers wisely avoided any such thing that they considered to be oppression. Under Article VIII of the Articles of Confederation, the United States Federal government did not have the power to tax income. All such power remained with the states. The United States Constitution, adopted in 1787, authorized the Congress to lay and collect taxes, but required that tax revenues be uniform, which excluded any kind of tax on individual income. **Tariffs** were the principal Federal tax through the

1800s. A **tariff** is a tax on imports or exports, in other words, on goods that move from one place to another.

The US Constitution says: In Article I Section 2 clause 3:

> *"Representatives and direct taxes shall be apportioned among the several States which may be included within this Union, according to their respective Numbers…*
> *Article I, Section 8, Clause 1:*
> *The Congress shall have power to lay and collect Taxes, Duties, Imposts and Excises...but all Duties, Imposts and Excises shall be uniform throughout the United States...*
> *Article I, Section 9, Clause 4:*
> *No Capitation (*a tax of a portioned, fixed amount per individual*) or other direct, Tax shall be laid, unless in proportion to the Census or Enumeration herein before directed to be taken."*

By 1796, state and local governments in fourteen of the 15 states taxed land. Delaware taxed the income from property. By the 1860s, the principle of **taxation of property** at a uniform rate had developed, and the states relied on property taxes as a major source of revenue.

The first Federal income tax was adopted as part of the **Revenue Act of 1861.** The tax lapsed after the American Civil War. Income taxes were held to be unconstitutional by the Supreme Court.

Hungry for money, in **1894 Congress enacted a flat rate Federal income tax**. It was ruled unconstitutional the following year by the U.S. Supreme

Court because it was a direct tax not apportioned according to the population of each state.

In **1909, President William Howard Taft** in an address to Congress, **proposed a 2% federal income tax** on corporations by way of an excise tax, and a constitutional amendment to allow the previously enacted income tax.

The congress passed then sent out the **16th amendment** in 1909 to the state governments for ratification by the state legislatures. There were forty-eight states at that time, and three-fourths, or 36, of them were needed to give their approval for it to be ratified. The process took until 1913.

Secretary of State Philander Knox received responses from forty-two states when he declared the 16th amendment ratified on February 25, 1913. Recent investigation into the state legislature voting process casts serious suspicion on that voting process.

In **1913, the 16th Amendment** was ratified, permitting the Federal government to levy an income tax. It defined income using language from prior laws.

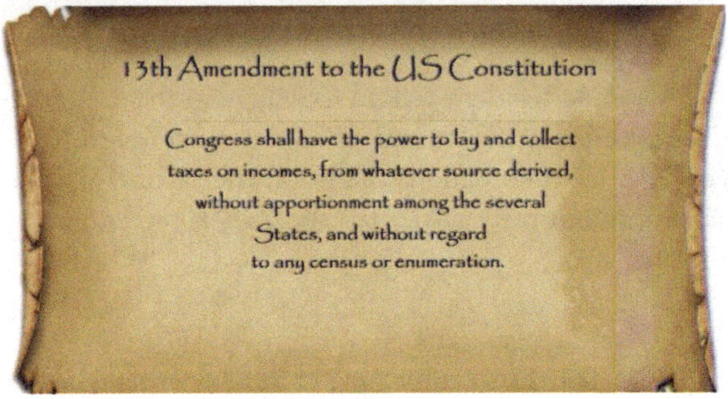

"When there is an income tax, the just man will pay more and the unjust less on the same amount of income." Plato said, over 2,300 years ago.

Plato was right. Americans can and do cheat on the income tax at every opportunity. Even the Attorney General, under President Obama "forgot" to report a $50,000 income.

The 16th amendment brought dramatic changes to American life.

- When adopted it set a **1% Tax rate** for incomes between $4,000 and $20,000.
- 1918 average family income was less than $3,000.00 per year.
- The rate for highest income was **3%**.
- The entire tax code was 15 pages.

By World War I, 1918, the tax had swelled to:
6% at the low end
and **77%** for top earners.

Under President Calvin Coolidge in the 1920s the rates were reduced to 3% and 25% respectively, which prevented a recession and brought on the "**Roaring 20s**" with great economic prosperity especially for average Americans.

Today the tax rate is
10% for those making $11,925.00 or less.
37% for those making $627,000.00 or more.

That does not include Social Security taken from every worker's check. **Social Security** is tricky. The government does not call it a tax; they call it insurance. It is forcibly taken from pay at the rate of 7.5%, but the employer pays an additional **7.5% for a 15% total**. What the government did was make it look like the nice employer pays half of the Social Security. Remember SAP? The employer may send the money to Washington for the worker, but the employer counts that money as an expense of hiring that employee. The employer knows it is a trick. Most employees don't see the trick unless they become self-employed, then they pay the whole 15% themselves. That is fifteen cents of every dollar made before any tax is paid.

But that's not all! There are more taxes: Medicaid taxes, property taxes, State income tax and sales taxes, excise taxes, import taxes, and TA DA! Gasoline taxes.

On average across the various states, the oil companies make $.08 per gallon, and the government makes $.18 in taxes on the same gallon. The states add an average of $.31 per gallon. That means 15% of the cost of a gallon of gas goes to the various taxes.

The original federal tax code was 27 pages long. The current federal income tax code is 74,608 pages, 187% the original size.

The truth is, the average American spends almost half of their work time earning money to pay taxes.

The Tax Foundation, an independent organization, estimates the number of days the average American family will work just to pay their federal, State and local tax burden in 2026 at 107 days. It is called Tax

Freedom Day. This compares with 22 days back in the early 1900s, before the income tax.

In a family where both parents work, often one parent basically works to pay the taxes since about a third of income goes to pay taxes.

It is no comfort to know that the US Government is spending money at a much higher, faster rate than it collects taxes.

Money not eaten by taxes gets eaten by the hidden tax: **INFLATION.**

Understanding inflation is easy. The only way money can become inflated is if a government prints more money than they can back with precious metal.

What is it worth if it is just printed paper?

Notice as inflation grows the

economy shrinks. That is because people are not as dumb as governments. Governments print paper money to pay debts. People raise prices to make up for the loss in value of the currency. These higher prices are the result of inflation. You may hear people say inflation is when prices go up. They are wrong, prices rising is the result of inflation. The source of inflation is always the same: an excess of printed currency.

In the 1970s Sheik Yamani of Saudi Arabia came to the United States. He was asked why a barrel of oil had

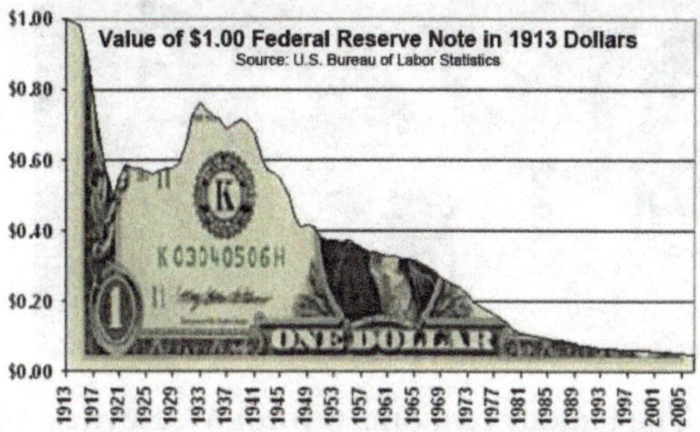

become so expensive. His answer was shocking. He pointed out that one ounce of gold could buy a barrel of oil, as was the case ten years before. Unfortunately, it took more dollars to buy that ounce of gold than ten years before. The reason it took more dollars to buy the barrel was our government's fault, not his. The real price of oil had not changed, our inflated dollar was just worth less.

Inflation did not begin in America. Remember the story about the Roman government trimming coins to make more coins with the same amount of gold. They also added less valuable metal to increase the money supply. Yeap! It caused inflation. People knew the money was not worth as much, so they raised their prices to make up for the loss. Uh oh, SAP factor at work.

One of the most famous cases of inflation occurred after the First World War in Germany. The German government printed massive amounts of money to cover debts. The German Mark fell so low in value that a man taking a wheelbarrow full of money to buy a loaf of bread was robbed. The thief dumped out the money and took the wheelbarrow because it had value, the money did not.

The famous economist, **John M. Keynes** said,

"There is no subtler, no surer means of overturning the existing basis of society than to inflate the currency. The process engages all the hidden forces of economic law on the side of destruction and does it in a manner which not one man in a million is able to diagnose".

Many people do not realize that **inflation is a hidden tax**. It especially taxes the poor. Inflation reduces the buying power of money, making everyone poorer. People with the least amount of money are hurt most. All have less because of what the government has taken in a hidden tax. The SAP factor cannot be cheated by the printing press.

Suppose the inflation rate is 3.5% per year. A person saving $30,000.00 in ten years inflation will reduce its buying power to $20,550.00 worth of goods or services.

If the inflation rate is 5.5% per year, that $30,000.00 will be worth only $16,650 in ten years. The loss is the same as if the money were taxed at that rate, hence a hidden tax.

For a specific example, a person with an income of $50,000.00 a year in 2012 needs to make $63,500.00 per year now to stay economically even because of inflation.

The government does not suffer from inflation. It costs little to print money, and a $500-dollar bill prints as fast as a one-dollar bill. The government uses printed money to pay its bills. The SAP factor will eventually catch up with government too.

The Debt Monster

Governments can legislate themselves into greater debt. At the printing of this book the **US National debt**

was **38 trillion dollars**. The National debt is the sum of all outstanding money owed by the Federal Government. Other long, technical, often misleading definitions amount to the sum of what our government owes.

Have some fun. Go to **www.debtclock.com**.watch the American debt grow.

Be sure to look at the button at the bottom that says, "**US unfunded Liabilities**". Those are financial promises to pay that are not due now but will be due. Money the government does not have. The promises are mostly to Social Security, Medicare, Medicaid, and other entitlement programs.

Soon the interest payments on our loan will be bigger than any other item in our budget. Eventually, all we will do is pay the interest payment, and we won't have any money left over for anything else. This situation is known as bankruptcy.

Each year since 1969, Congress has spent more money than its income. The Treasury Department borrows money to meet Congress's appropriations. A little more than $11 trillion is owed to foreign and domestic investors. The rest is caused by the Federal Reserve, which buys congressional debt with checks made from thin air to drag down interest rates through quantitative easing. ***Quantitative easing* is fancy term for printing large amounts of currency with no intrinsic value**; it is inflation.

Business Behavior

This is the popular image of the two forces on Wall Street, the home of the New York Stock Exchange.

If it is a "**bull**" **market**, profits and prices are up along with stock value. In a **"bear" market**, prices, profits, and stock values fall. The amazing part is that good things can happen in either a "bull" or a "bear" market. It comes down to understanding what it takes to start and maintain a business.

Suppose for a moment that you were going to start a business. You decide you are so good at making "blue light computer enhancements" that you want to try to make a real business of it. You have been selling them to friends and family, who put you in contact with others bringing good sales. Price has been no problem. So far you have made the BLCEs yourself in your basement in your spare time.

You start a business web site and advertise in a local paper that results in more orders. After a few weeks, the web site is getting ten to twenty inquiries a day. You hire a couple of friends part time to help make the BLCEs while you respond to customers and fill orders. A month later it happens; in one day, you receive 340 orders.

Using your savings and borrowing from relatives you move to an available building, improve your production method, and find three full-time people to assemble the BLCEs. Filling the orders continues to be a challenge, and much of your time is taken up dealing with customers and organizing your operation. Orders continue to pile up.

It is time to quit your regular job to devote full time to this growing business. When you review the bookkeeping, you find more is being spent on rent, heat, wages, materials, and shipping than you imagined. If you do quit your job, you will take a huge pay cut. The orders keep pouring in at ever higher numbers. You leave your job and throw yourself into your business.

The BLCEs have now attracted international attention, bringing a flood of orders beyond your capability to produce. Then you find an automated system that will vastly increase your output. It will cost hundreds of thousands of dollars.

A bank friend agrees to propose to his board the idea of lending these funds you want if you can supply a business plan to prove your capability to repay the loan. He insists you incorporate and hire a lawyer too. This new activity causes you to hire a supervisor also to oversee the production you are too busy to watch yourself anymore. You also hire a personal assistant to help you stay organized and on top of orders, while you incorporate and prepare the business plan for the bank.

The presentation to the bank board goes well, except they insist you move to a larger building to have the room to install the new equipment. The new building lease changes your cash flow requiring more investment from the bank. Now, you must find a building you can purchase and prepare a new presentation for the bank. Then, the bank claims the amount needed is too high based on the projected income of your business.

Your new lawyer finds a friend who will provide a building for a percentage of the business. The investor providing the building gets a fifteen percent share of your business. The bank now gives you the loan, and you move into the building and install the new equipment.

You are now seriously behind in filling orders. To catch up you hire more people and add a second shift with an additional supervisor. The cost of all this has put the business at a slight loss that you hope to make up for with higher production in the coming year.

As the business stabilizes you notice that the orders have levelled out as well. Over the next few months orders decline. A little investigation reveals that a big corporation has produced an imitation of your BLCEs with more features at a lower price.

You begin research to find out what they are doing and how they do it. In the meantime, you lower your price to hold the business you have.

In all of this, your personal income has not changed. You are still making much less than you did before you left your regular job. Is this fun or what?

Making the changes necessary to catch up to your competition will take more money for production changes. The bank is not interested in lending it to you. Desperate to get the competitive advantage, you get a second mortgage on your house to get the money.

Before you set up the revised production you discover your employees want to form a union. You believe this can be avoided by dealing directly with them, but your lawyer informs you that you cannot interfere in any way with union organization. He tells you that you cannot even bring the subject up with them under the labor laws.

Your employees vote in a union that sits down with you to discuss work conditions and wages. They want higher pay, fewer hours, overtime pay, health care insurance, seven paid holidays, and double time for workers working holidays, better bathrooms, a cafeteria, and a paved parking lot. If you don't agree to these demands, they plan to strike. You negotiate as best you can to keep the plant running, agreeing to much of the demands.

Bookkeeping shows that you are losing money. The bank is not pleased. It demands you come up with a solution.

In the meantime, you have developed a new BLCE superior to any on the market that can be produced at a much lower price. Installing the changes in the current union plant will absorb most of the cost gains. You decide to move the new production to another state under a separate corporation your lawyer creates.

This new plant produces a better product at a lower cost with fewer, non-union workers. You let the original plant operate until the bank payments for the original production line are paid. Then, since the plant is at a financial loss, you allow it to slow until it has so little business you can close it.

In the new state, the Environmental Protection Agency files a complaint against your operation demanding air and water purification measures with financial penalties until the changes are approved by EPA. The problem was left by the previous owner. Now you know why he gave you such a good deal on the building.

For a couple of years, you struggled on fighting against even more competition, unable to raise prices. Until a friend puts you in contact with a Mexican businessman who suggests you move most of your production to Mexico. You don't want to do that, yet the cost of operating there will finally give you the competitive advantage your business needs to survive.

The operation you set up in Mexico is so successful your competition offers to buy your company. Selling the company will give you financial independence for the rest of your life. You sell out and enter early retirement.

Being a millionaire prevents you from working anymore since your money puts you in a position to be sued by opportunists. Lawsuits are always filed against the wealthy.

Relaxing on the beach one day you read an article online about you and your business behavior; it is about your greed, how badly you treated the union, how you closed a perfectly good plant, threw dozens out of work, your EPA violations, and your lack of care for the environment. It tells how you moved your business to Mexico cheating more Americans out of jobs, then sold your operations to an international conglomerate for big bucks. You are criticized for selfish, greedy, miserly, ruthless, business behavior.

Congratulations, sport, and welcome to the club.

To survive every business must make more money than it spends.

Businesses do not exist to provide jobs, pay taxes, preserve the environment, hand out employee benefits, or enhance their local community. Those things are the natural outgrowth of a successful business, not its purpose. If a business does not produce money it dies. Those who have never run a business never see this truth.

It is not evil, greedy, or selfish to make money. Those are human failings common to all of us in one measure or another: rich or poor, running a business, or as an employee.

Companies constantly seek lower cost ways to make products, which benefits customers. Companies constantly seek ways to increase profits. The critics of the 'big profits' often own the stocks on which dividends are paid based on profit. The whole operation of the New York Stock Exchange and other stock markets lives and dies by profit share. When profits are up, stocks are up and vice versa.

The health of the economy is measured to a large degree by how well the stock market does. There are millions of owners of company stocks. Millions of people benefit or lose depending on whether the company stock they own makes a profit or not.

Market participants include individual retail investors, institutional investors such as mutual funds, banks, insurance companies and hedge funds, also publicly traded corporations trading in their own shares. Studies have suggested that institutional investors and corporations trading in their own shares generally receive higher risk-adjusted returns than individual investors. That means they are paid more to take higher risks than the average stock purchaser.

Statistics show that in recent decades stocks have made up a large proportion of the financial assets of the average household. This benefit comes mostly from financial investment in the form of various kinds of institutional portfolios for groups of individuals, such as pension funds, mutual funds, hedge funds, and insurance investment programs.

Every situation provides an opportunity for those smart enough to take advantage of it. Money made from the stock market depends on overall good market performance. This means companies need to make strong profits, which depend on good production decisions, good product development decisions, and using the instruments of production to maximize income.

The nature of business behavior is making money. The benefactor of that behavior is always the customer. The perfect example is Apple Inc, that created the iPad, iPhone, iPod, the MacBook. A company, like many others, that produces better products at much lower prices than they did ten years ago.

Customers want the best product at the lowest price.
Good producers lower prices to get more sales and increase profit.

Governments and Money

Not recommended for younger audiences.

> **"The first lesson of economics is scarcity**: There is never enough of anything to satisfy all those who want it. The first lesson of politics is to disregard the first lesson of economics."
> — *Thomas Sowell*

All the governments of the world of whatever time or sort, monarchy, republic, and communist, have made the same mistakes with money. They all spend more than they have.

Running a government takes money. Giving money to the government is worse than giving it to a spoiled child. The more it has the more it screams for more. Unlike the spoiled child, the government can do harm to those who refuse to give.

The reason governments give for their greed is always the same, "that it is for the governed." Even dictators make this altruistic claim. The problem governments have with money is that they do not earn any. They do not work, and they create nothing. They receive funds on demand for any reason they deem important. Unlike a business, they neither fear monetary loss nor fear spending too much. The result is they both create debt and spend too much.

The difference in the use of money between oppressive governments and those of free people is that a dictatorial state controls with fear and free countries control with money.

> "The American Republic will endure until the day Congress discovers that it can bribe the public with the public's money."
>
> Alexis de Tocqueville

Republics find that offering money as an incentive in place of a law allows them to avoid violating their own constitution. They offer money for roads if a certain speed and design is followed. They offer money to schools if certain performance requirements are met. Money from the state always has strings attached. For many years the State of Alabama received no federal funds because it refused to follow the federal requirements attached.

The constitution gives the power of the government purse to congress. The House of Representatives is where all revenue bills must originate. Anything having to do with government spending, or taxes, begins with congress.

In the 1960s the U. S. Federal government developed social programs to eliminate poverty. These became known as entitlement programs. **Entitlements** are laws based on **social equality** or **enfranchisement.** They are a false extension of God given rights to life, liberty, and the pursuit of happiness. Social Security, Medicare, and Medicaid are the major entitlement programs today.

Under an entitlement program the government spends as much as is needed, year to year regardless of budget. This means that no one has financial control of entitlement spending.

The **Budget Process** of the United States does not work like a business. Any business estimates what the sales for the coming year will be. Based on that income expectation, the business determines their projected expenses and possible profit. If the sales are expected to decline, the business reduces its expenses.

The government simply looks at each department's request for money and proposes a budget based on the requests. Naturally, every department asks for increases each year. Once budget needs are established, anything less than what is requested is considered a budget cut. Using this method, the government never reduces spending even with their so called "budget cuts".

The process called **"Baseline budgeting"** is one of many ways that politicians claim to cut spending when they are increasing spending. For example, if an agency's budget is projected to increase by $100 million, and congress allows only $75 million, according to baseline budgeting, that agency had a $25 million cut. No business could forecast they want to spend $100,000 but budget only $75,000 and say they have saved $25,000. A business can only save by spending less than spent previously.

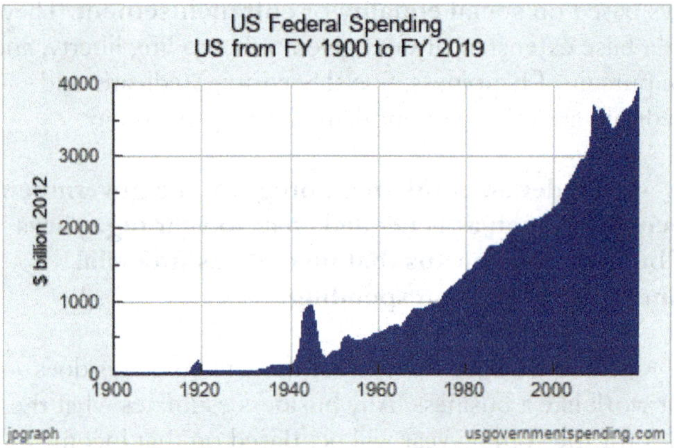

Baseline budgeting gives politicians an opportunity to deceive taxpayers by allowing congress to claim that they are holding the line on spending while providing more services. The result is that government spending has never decreased.

Every round of budget negotiations involves baseline budgeting with both political parties complaining that the other party is using the process to mask spending increases.

When the congress reports a budget cut it does not mean that they are spending less. The new budgets have been higher every year, no matter how "big" the cuts. Study the chart on the previous page and see if you can find any cuts.

To protect America from financial collapse congress created the **Federal Reserve System**, or the **Federal Reserve**, and informally called the **Fed.** It is the central banking system of the United States. It was created on December 23, 1913, with the enactment of the Federal Reserve Act. This happened as a response to a series of financial panics, particularly a severe panic in 1907. America was bailed out of the 1907 panic by J. P. Morgan. It frightened congress to know that one man could control so much financial power.

The Fed is a private bank owned by international bankers, many who are not known to us.

The task of the Federal Reserve System is to ensure the money supply, maintain employment, keep prices stable, and keep interest rates at a moderate level by regulating monetary policy.

Components of the Federal Reserve System also supervise banks, provide financial services, and conduct research on the United States economy and the economies in the surrounding region.

The original central bank established by the founders was abandoned under President Andrew Jackson in 1836. He was the only president to completely pay of off the national debt. After President Jackson ended the central bank America operated without a central bank until 1913.

Senate Republican leader **Nelson Aldrich** secretly arranged the meeting of international bankers who actually planned the Federal Reserve Bank at a hidden resort on Jekyll Island off the coast of Georgia. He then presented this plan as a bill before congress.

In truth, the bill before congress was the work of the most influential bankers in the world. They would become the controllers of the new central bank, the

Federal Reserve. Under the pretense of government reform, they took control of US money.

Congress passed **Federal Reserve Act** in **1913**, under the President **Woodrow Wilson**. It required two of the board of directors to come from US government. Banks all over the country hurried to join the Federal Reserve System. All these banks then came under the control of the Central Bank. They could no longer set rates of interest on their own. The Fed would do that and more.

Notably, the **Federal Reserve Bank is not part of the Federal Government**, nor does the government control it. It is controlled by the board of directors made up of international money interests.

The main purpose of the Federal Reserve is to protect the economy of the United States, maintain an even flow of money to provide funds when the banking system falters. It makes one wonder why in the economic crisis of 1929 the Federal Reserve did nothing? What the Federal Reserve does is control of the American economy.

The Congress established three objectives for economic policy in 1913, maximum employment, stable prices, and moderate interest rates. They placed the responsibility for these objectives with the Federal Reserve. The first two objectives are sometimes referred to as the Federal Reserve's dual mandate.

With all their control, the FED takes no responsibility for the condition of the economy.

Isn't it interesting that the central bank working for our government has never been audited? ***Audit*: a formal examination of an organization's accounts or financial situation.** These are required by law with all other financial institutions.

All governments have only one source of income: taxation. When the government spends too much, it is the citizens who pay. Government handles money shortages by increasing taxes, but it never cuts spending. No business or household treats money the way the government does.

"There are severe limits for what a government can do for an economy, but there are almost no limits to the harm it can do".
Milton Friedman

Economic Cycles and Depression

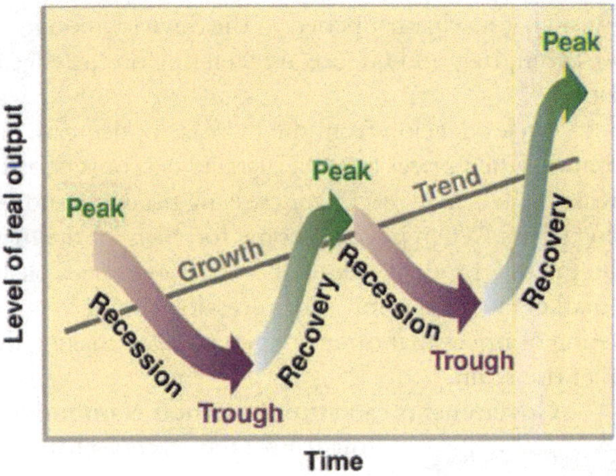

There is a variation in the flow of the economy, a sort of wave pattern, as the exchange of money and goods rises and falls. It would be surprising if it was always the same. It looks like the diagram above. The terms shown are economic terms. Inventing terms and definitions and making them complex keeps economists in business.

The cause for this ebb and flow of business is related to the growth of GDP, household income, employment rates, inflation, and the central bank control of money.

GDP, or Gross Domestic Product, refers to the market value of all goods and services produced within a country in a given period, usually per calendar year.

Because business cycles are split into two parts they might be called bicycles but are not. There is an up part, and a down part to the cycle. In a healthy economy, the cycles are regular with a trend upward. If the trend begins to descend the economy has an economic problem that must be corrected to change the trend. If a downward trend continues, the economy may collapse as well as the government.

That is what happened to the Soviet Union in 1990. Spain, Italy and Greece are teetering on the edge of collapse.

Cycles develop from the increase or decrease in **demand**. When prices become attractive to buyers, sales increase. Sellers may react by increasing products and raising prices. When prices become too high, or the market is too full of a product, sales fall. The drop in sales pushes the market into **recession**. The recession results in a lowering of prices that often spurs new sales, making the market rise again.

Governments can **stimulate their economies by lowering taxes.** It does happen. Lower taxes cause people to spend more money for products and services, causing an economic rise called a **boom**.

President John F. Kennedy did this in the 1960s. He lowered taxes. People spent more money in the markets which resulted in an increase in business which increased federal revenues. President Kennedy understood a lower percent tax would make more money for the government, because it is not the percentage, it is the number of times the dollar gets taxed that tax creates more revenue. If a dollar is taxed less, it is spent more often. When a dollar is spent more often it produces more revenue.

In the 1980s, President Ronald Reagan lowered taxes. The result was increasing federal revenue, despite the entitlement programs that the Kennedy administration did not have in the 1960s.

The Great Depression

Economies that continue in a downturn can move from a **recession** to a **depression**. Depression is noted by extensive unemployment, widespread banking failures, a large number of bankruptcies, and a very small money supply.

In 1930 America entered an economic depression accompanied by most of the western world economies. What happened is frequently made more complex than is necessary. It is not hard to understand depression. For many Americans it meant job loss, and the loss of their home because they could not pay their mortgage. Many had to depend on handouts to survive.

This picture is of a Detroit "soup kitchen" that provided food to the unemployed during the great depression of the 1930s.

The depression began when the stock market experienced a severe drop in stock prices. The drop caused stockholders to panic and sell more stock causing further losses and more panic. The result was a **stock market crash**.

Since banks had also invested large portions of their clients' savings in the stock market, these banks were forced to close when the stock market crashed. Bank closings caused another panic across the country. Afraid they would lose their savings, people rushed to withdraw their money. The massive withdrawals worsened the money shortage causing additional banks to close. The money supply was in trouble.

Back in 1913 the federal government created the **Federal Reserve** to make sure the money supply did not fail to support the economy. The Federal Reserve ignored the money shortage in the 1930s creating the Great Depression. The Nobel Prize winner for economics, Milton Friedman, points out that no matter what faults investors, banks or industry might be accused of it was the Federal Reserve that brought on the Great Depression.

During the first years of the depression, 1929-1933 the amount of money in the United States declined by one third, the total number of banks declined by one third. The Federal Reserve had enough currency to end the downturn but did nothing. Even when the bankers and congress pleaded for the Federal Reserve to step in, they did nothing. It was the responsibility of the Federal Reserve to resolve shortages in the money supply.

The government caused the economic disaster of the 1930s, which in turn blamed business for the problem. Sound familiar? If the economy does well the Federal Reserve takes credit for it because of its good financial policies. If the economy falters, the Federal Reserve says, 'in spite of our best efforts the businesses of the country have ruined things again.' In the entire history of the Federal Reserve, they have never been responsible for the economic woes of America.

The Great Depression devastated the world economy. Prices dropped; business plunged by more than half. Unemployment in the U.S. rose to 25%. Cities across the globe suffered, especially those dependent on heavy industry. Construction halted in many countries. Farming and rural areas suffered as crop prices fell by 60%.

It is often stated that President **Franklin Delano Roosevelt** was responsible for the economic recovery, that FDR "**saved capitalism from itself**" through social programs. Roosevelt did look for a solution when he became President. He thought he found it in **John Maynard Keynes.**

Keynes solution to the Great Depression was to stimulate the economy by a reduction in interest rates and **government investment in infrastructure.** Government spending would inject money into the economy, he argued; people would spend the money at businesses that then invest in expansion. The initial stimulation starts a cascade of spending, resulting in economic activity that grows from the original spending. Notice, his plan was to do all this with the the existing amount of wealth or abundance.

Of course, to spend the government must take the money from its only source, the people. The government can tax the people, borrow money, or print money. In any case, the people under the government end up paying the bill. No government can create prosperity by spending, any more than a household or business can create prosperity by spending.

The effect of FDR's social programs lengthened and deepened the depression. Shortly after Roosevelt's inauguration in 1933, drought and erosion combined to cause the **Dust Bowl**, displacing thousands from their farms in the west.

Roosevelt argued that restructuring the economy would prevent further depression. His **New Deal** programs were supposed to create demand and provide work for the impoverished through increased government spending and financial reforms.

Reform of the economy was the goal of the **National Recovery Act (NIRA)** of 1933. It tried to end so called "cutthroat competition" by forcing industries to come up with codes that established the rules of operation for all firms within specific industries, such as minimum prices, agreements not to compete, and production restrictions. The NIRA was found to be unconstitutional by unanimous decision of the U.S. Supreme Court on May 27, 1935.

Social Security

Playing on a myth that American business failed to provide for the common man, and that government must step in to protect the 'little fellow, Roosevelt introduced Social Security. The practice of protecting the 'little fellow' is often called **'social justice.'** It is also a myth that these government programs result from public demand. Social Security is a government program, dreamed up by well-meaning bureaucrats with no public demand, none at all.

The Social Security Act attempted to limit the dangers of life: old age, poverty, unemployment, and the burdens of widows and fatherless children. **Social Security** refers to the **1935 federal Old-Age, Survivors, and Disability Insurance** program. It bears no resemblance to insurance.

Real insurance protects the financial well-being of an individual, or company, in case of a potential loss. It is offered in exchange for premium payments of a specified amount over a specified period. The offer is similar for all who choose to buy it.

Social Security comes from payroll taxes through the **Federal insurance Contributions Act (FICA).** The word 'contribution' makes it sound voluntary; it is not. It is required as part of taxation on paycheck earnings up to a certain amount. It is a **regressive tax** of 15% of income. It is regressive because the poorest paid workers pay the highest percentage of their income.

In 2010 Social Security was payable on the first $106,800 of income. Those making more than that stopped paying once their annual income went above $106.800. A person making $106,800 paid $16,020 to FICA that year, while the person making $200,000 or

$300,000 or a million dollars paid no more than $16,020 to FICA that year.

To disguise the high percentage of the tax, the Federal government came up with the idea of making the employer pay half of the tax prior to paying the employee. Employees drawing a paycheck never see the 15%, they only see half, 7.5%, withdrawn from their pay. The employer hiring a person at $30,000 a year sees that employee costing him $32,250 because he will pay $2,250 direct to the government in addition to the salary. Those who are self-employed see the trick because they pay 15% of every dollar of income to Social Security.

Note: Investment income that pays interest or dividends does not require Social Security payments.

What is never mentioned about the Social Security Act is the vast increase in funds it brought to the federal government. In a single sweep of supposed generous legislation the government tripled its income.

Roosevelt knew he could pass new laws faster than the Supreme Court could find them unconstitutional. He would have a new one ready before the old ones bit the dust. The new laws grew the power of unions. The expanding number of union members provided votes for Roosevelt.

By 1936, the economy recovered much of the loss of 1929, except unemployment remained at 11 per cent.

In June 1937, the Roosevelt administration cut spending and increased taxes to balance the federal budget. The American economy buckled and declined for over a year. Industrial production dropped about 30 %.

The blatantly socialist, unconstitutional programs of FDR did not end the depression. Neither did World

War II that brought on an even wilder spree of spending than the government had during the 1930s.

At the end of the war, 1945, millions of returning soldiers found jobs, bought or built houses, bought clothes, cars, appliances, and other goods in an avalanche of buying.

At the same time, the government cut spending by 75%. The US federal budget went from a deficit of over 21% to a surplus of 1.7% in two years. Unemployment fell to 3.5%, normal for a healthy economy. The dramatic spending cuts and small tax reductions boosted economic growth that would continue to the end of the century.

Riding the cycles. Economic cycles have two parts: **Boom and Bust.** People, rich or poor, who go through a boom-and-bust cycle, with minimum damage, are either lucky or smart. It is better to be smart than depend on luck. People who are able ride through these cycles unharmed don't have large debts. Debt makes any loss in income or investment harder. Debt is always what drives bankruptcy. No one can go bankrupt if they don't owe any money.

Smart people have a **budget** and stick to it. They also save money and invest. The budget keeps them from having a growing debt. When hard economic times come they are in a strong position. A budget would be a wonderful idea for the government too. Governments prefer to trust luck.

The average American household has $15,000.00 of credit card debt on one or more cards. The rate of interest monthly on the balance is 14%. That works out to $2,100.00 a year in **interest** alone. In the event of job loss, if the credit card payments cannot be made the credit card company will ask for the entire amount. If the cardholder does not pay that, the credit card company may sue for payment by taking the funds through the court. In these cases, the court may award the property of the cardholder to the credit card company. This is why credit card debt is the worst debt one can have. Successfully riding the economic cycle requires minimum debt, none when possible.

Smart people also invest and save. Every household needs a certain amount of money saved for emergencies. They also should invest in or buy a **commodity** that will return more than it costs over a period of time. It could be **stocks**, **bonds** or precious metals.

People who invest know the **rule of 72.** You may recall from earlier in the book it is mathematical rule used to find the number of years it takes an investment to double in value. It is calculated by dividing 72 by the annual rate of return. An investment earning 10% annually will double the investor's funds in 72 divided by 10, or 7.2 years.

This is important because inflation will eat some of the gain. A person investing $10,000.00 at 7.2% in 2001 will double the investment in 2011, getting $20,000.00. Because of inflation, he will have lost 20% of the original buying power of the 2001 money, or $4,000.00. In truth, his money does not double, since twice $10,000.00 in the 2001-dollar value would be $24,000.00 in 2011, corrected for inflation.

Economics and Law

There are two forms of law, or two legal systems, to which governments submit themselves: **Natural Law** and **Civil Law.** The one they choose often determines their economic vitality and power.

Natural Law, often called common law. or man understanding that law is based upon the law of God. In natural law the solid foundation of the scripture forms the basis on which all laws are made. The basic principles of natural law cannot be changed.

In the Declaration of Independence, the reference to
… *"certain inalienable rights to life, liberty and the pursuit of happiness"* …
was directly from natural law.
This was a concept the British founded as part of their **English Common Law**.

Under Natural Law individual rights and freedom are understood to come from God, not the state. The establishment of natural law here on earth comes from heaven. Such law is fixed, it never changes, it supersedes all time, and whatever changes a society may experience. The law of God is perfect in nature, a solid rock upon which natural law is built.

Civil Law comes from Roman law. It was put into a code by Emperor Justinian in 534 A.D.

Justinian commissioned a legal expert to gather all the legal notes, commentaries, and laws of the Roman legal system into a single text: this was the *Codex Iustinianus* **or Justinian Code.**

It is law created by and for the state. He did a great job. Nations to this date look to the **Justinian Code** for creating law. This is where the concept of "innocent until proven guilty" comes from.

The weakness of Civil Law is that government is the ultimate authority. Individual freedom, or any human rights, is a gift from government. The rights a government gives under civil law can also be taken away by the government.

The growth of natural law made the countries that applied it wealthier. Beginning with England then the United States, prosperity became possible because of the freedoms enjoyed by their citizens. Some European countries followed this model too. They noted the ability of citizens to pursue their own interests caused them to become wealthy, in turn causing their country to share in their gain.

In the late 1800s, ideas of socialism crept in to many societies. Socialism adheres to civil law. Under socialism the object of interest is the welfare of the state, not the freedom of the individual. As socialism grew, the prosperity of the countries using it declined. The Soviet Socialist Republics collapsed economically because no individual had anything to gain by seeing customers provided with good, cheap products and services. Cuba faces the same problem today its economy is collapsed.

China, though communist, has decided to allow some private ownership to spur its economy. The Chinese understand that a measure of individual freedom must be given to citizens to accomplish their goals. They have had a movement back toward a free market. A movement driven by the desire to create wealth. Unfortunately, governments know that free markets cut into government control. China, using civil law is reversing free markets by imposing restrictive laws to protect their power. Many economic studies have shown how countries with civil law tend to protect their power, not their markets.

The more economic freedom a country has the more prosperous it tends to be. The following is a list of the top ten countries showing their rating of economic freedom.

The Heritage Foundation and the Wall Street Journal created the **Index of Economic Freedom**. According to Heritage, the creators of the Index took an approach similar to Adam Smith's *The Wealth of Nations*.

> *"Basic institutions that protect the liberty of individuals to pursue their own economic interests result in greater prosperity for the larger society".*

The Index of Economic Freedom scores nations on ten factors of economic freedom shown in the following list. They use statistics from major economic organizations including the World Bank, the International Monetary Fund, and the Economist Intelligence Unit.

Business Freedom: Business freedom is a quantitative measure of the ability to start, operate, and close a business that represents the overall burden of regulation as well as the efficiency of government in the regulatory process.

Trade Freedom: Trade freedom is a composite measure of the absence of tariff and non-tariff barriers that affect imports and exports of goods and services. Different imports entering a country can, and often do, face different tariffs.

Monetary Freedom: Monetary freedom combines a measure of price stability with an assessment of price controls. Both inflation and price controls distort market activity. Price stability without micro-economic intervention is the ideal state for the free market.

Government Size/Spending: This component considers the level of government expenditures as a percentage of GDP. Government expenditures, including consumption and transfers, account for the entire score.

Fiscal Freedom: Fiscal freedom is a measure of the tax burden imposed by the government.

Property Rights: The property rights component is an assessment of the ability of individuals to accumulate private property, secured by clear laws that are fully enforced by the state.

Investment Freedom: In an economically free country, there would be no constraints on the flow of investment capital. Individuals and firms would be allowed to move their resources into and out of specific activities internally and across the country's borders without restriction.

Financial Freedom: Financial freedom is a measure of banking efficiency as well as a measure of independence from government control and interference in the financial sector.

Freedom from Corruption: Corruption erodes economic freedom. The higher the level of corruption, the lower the level of overall economic freedom and the lower a country's score.

Labor Freedom: The labor freedom component is a quantitative measure that investigates aspects of the legal and regulatory framework of a country's labor market.

Index of Economic Freedom World Rankings

The numbers are: Overall score, Property Rights, Government integrity, Judicial Effectiveness

1. Singapore 83.5 -0.4 83.9 84.4 **Free**
2. Switzerland 83.0 -0.8 83.8 84.2 **Free**
3. Ireland 82.6 0.6 82.0 82.0 **Free**
4. Taiwan 80.0 -0.7 80.7 80.1 **Free**
5. Luxembourg 79.2 0.8 78.4 80.6 **Mostly Free**
6. Denmark 77.8 0.2 77.6 78.0 **Mostly Free**
7. New Zealand 77.8 -1.1 78.9 80.6 **Mostly Free**
8. Estonia 77.8 -0.8 78.6 80.0 **Mostly Free**
9. Sweden 77.5 77.5 77.9 **Mostly Free**
10. Norway 77.5 0.6 76.9 76.9 **Mostly Free**
11. Netherlands 77.3 -0.7 78.0 79.5 **Mostly Free**
12. Finland 76.3 -0.8 77.1 78.3 **Mostly Free**
13. Australia 76.2 1.4 74.8 77.7 **Mostly Free**
14. South Korea 73.1 -0.6 73.7 74.6 **Mostly Free**
15. Lithuania 72.9 0.7 72.2 75.8 **Mostly Free**
16. Canada 72.4 -1.3 73.7 76.6 **Mostly Free**
17. Cyprus 72.2 -0.1 72.3 72.9 **Mostly Free**
18. Germany 72.1 -1.6 73.7 76.1 **Mostly Free**
19. Latvia 71.5 -1.3 72.8 74.8 **Mostly Free**
20. Mauritius 71.5 0.9 70.6 70.9 **Mostly Free**
21. Chile 71.4 0.3 71.1 74.4 **Mostly Free**
22. United Arab Emirates 71.1 0.2 70.9 70.2 **Mostly Free**
23. Iceland 70.5 -1.7 72.2 77.0 **Mostly Free**
24. Czech Republic 70.2 -1.7 71.9 74.4 **Mostly Free**
25. United States 70.1 -0.5 70.6 72.1 **Mostly Free**

Notice that the United States is not the freest country according to the index. America's economic freedom remains only "mostly free," this year reaching one of the lowest ratings in the history of the Index at 70.2. The U.S. ranking has dwindled to 26th freest in the 2025 index, the worst position that the U.S. economy has ever held. The Biden administration's misguided anti-growth entrepreneurial policies and mounting deficit spending over the past four years resulted in this decline.

Singapore held its position as the world's most-free economy, Switzerland followed closely behind at second, and Ireland (3), Taiwan (4), and Luxembourg (5) rounded out the top five.

The Paraguayan economy has recorded one of the largest economic freedom score increases in the 2025 Index and has undergone a notable expansion. The reform-minded Santiago Peña administration, which took office in August 2023, has pursued a series of legislative reforms to improve the overall economic environment and generate job growth in numerous business areas.

North Korea, Cuba, Venezuela, Zimbabwe, and Sudan remained the world's least economically free nations.

This comparison of freedom now needs to be compared to the prosperity of the most economically free countries to see how they line up. The United States no longer makes the list of the 10 most prosperous countries in the world, according to a new study by the Legatum Institute. The **Legatum Prosperity Index** found that while prosperity increased globally, the U.S. fell to 17th place in its rankings, but first in business environment.

Top 10 Most Prosperous Countries (Legatum Prosperity Index 2023):

Denmark	1
Sweden	2
Norway	3
Finland	4
Switzerland	5
Netherlands	6
Luxembourg	7
Iceland	8
Germany	9
New Zealand	10

The Legatum Institute is part of the Legatum Group, a private investment company founded by New Zealand billionaire Christopher Chandler.

And the winners in the 2016 most prosperous race are...

Four Scandinavian countries top the list. While these countries follow a traditional Civil Law form it is interesting to note what they have done in recent years. Scandinavian countries slashed government budgets after the financial crisis of the early 1990s.

Netherlands and Switzerland are unique in the business world. Switzerland is the world's banker. They escaped the ravages of two world wars because no belligerent wanted to destroy the country holding the purse for everyone. Holland, a Civil Law country, has built its strength on international trade. The Dutch government has always depended on their merchants for survival. This puts interest in business ahead of interests in government power.

Luxembourg, number seven, is a stable and high-income economy with low inflation, and a high level of innovation. Unemployment is traditionally low, although it is affected by the global financial crisis. Luxembourg's economy has remained flat the last few years. In 2011, tiny Luxembourg was the second richest country in the world.

The United States, a Natural Law country, is 19th. The economy of the United States is the world's largest national economy and the world's second largest overall economy, the GDP of the European Union being approximately $2 trillion larger.

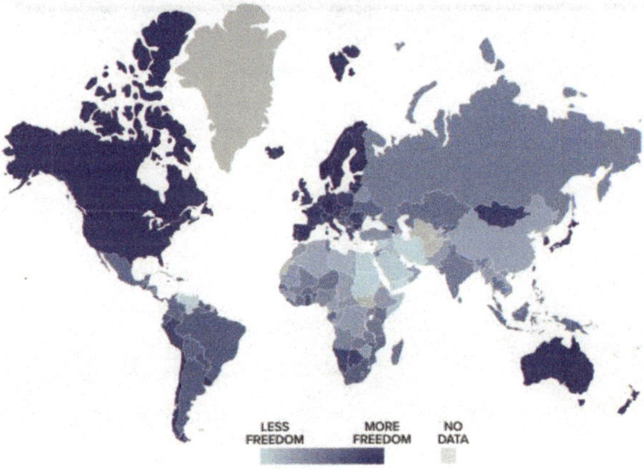

Finally, **The Human Freedom Index 2025** presents the state of human freedom in the world based on a broad measure that includes personal, civil, and economic freedom. The report is co-published by the Cato Institute and the Fraser Institute. This is shown to demonstrate the relationship between human freedom and economic prosperity.

The Basic comparison:

Natural Law
Based on unchangeable principles from God.

Civil Law
Created by government for specific purposes.

Getting Rich Quick
And other Lies

This chapter covers the most common lies put forward by individuals unwilling to accept the evidence set plainly before them.

There is a saying, **"If it sounds too good to be true it probably is not true".** Get rich quick schemes rarely work as advertised. It is fascinating to watch **infomercials** by people who claim to have made large sums of money. They speak about how eager they are to help you make tons of money too. Just follow the simple plan that they have made so that you can easily make fifty, sixty or two-hundred thousand dollars. You must ask yourself, what is this person going to gain from this deal? They always have something you need to buy to get in on the scheme. What they are really telling you is that there is a lot of money in making infomercials.

> *"Dishonest money dwindles away, but he who gathers money little by little makes it grow."*
> *Proverbs 13:11*

Following is a list of lies people too often believe.

Lie #1, Government control and spending create prosperity.

In the 1930s Americans insisted the government do something about the Great Depression. President Franklin Roosevelt introduced the "New Deal," a set of sweeping changes to the economy. A law was passed to stop employers from firing workers. The Employers went bankrupt following the law, then no one had a job.

The government then stopped foreign companies from importing to America so that Americans could make those products here. Unable to make those products here, more businesses went bankrupt creating more unemployment.

Then the government set up government work programs for the unemployed. Millions of Americans joined these work forces, building the Hoover Dam, the Golden Gate Bridge, and the Tennessee Valley Authority water projects. The government spent billions paying for material and labor on these projects. Ten years later, the U.S. debt had grown, and unemployment was worse than at the beginning in 1930.

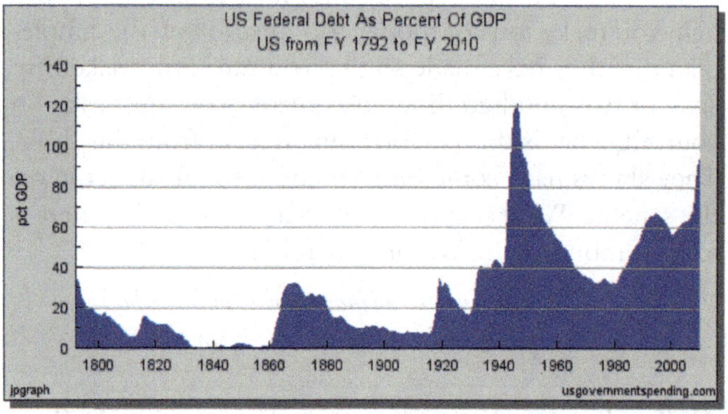

These schemes violate the economic SAP factor.

Look at the chart above showing federal debt as a percentage of GDP. Notice the big jump about 1918, which was from the cost of World War I. Then see how it jumps again starting in 1930 as the federal programs of the Depression began. Then comes the huge leap in the 1940s, that is the cost of World War II. It grew larger than our GDP.

From 1945 to 1980, the debt steadily declined. This happened because the costs of the war effort disappeared. Also, the government programs of the depression were gone. Government spending fell. Soldiers coming home started buying houses, clothes and food. Business grew, employment grew, which stimulated more growth. The 'baby boom" began, the largest increase in birth rate in US history. It created more demand for consumer products, more jobs and the GDP grew, and the debt went down.

Look at the last steep climb in US debt beginning about 2009. That is from the "stimulus," or **The American Recovery and Reinvestment Act of 2009.** This was done to create jobs, infrastructure investment, energy efficiency and science, assistance to the unemployed, State, and local fiscal stabilization, for the fiscal year 2009, Do you wonder who is going to pay for that? The fact is, you are, just as soon as you start working and earning a wage. Uncle Sam will deduct it from your income.

> *"Loading up the nation with debt and leaving it for the following generations to pay is morally irresponsible."*
>
> *Thomas Jefferson*

The American Recovery Act was followed by TARP. TARP Act allowed the US government to reimburse banks for losses caused by the massive failure of mortgage loans given to people who defaulted on their loans. Instead of allowing the banks to fail, the government decided to save them with billions of dollars. Those billions must come from taxpayers: SAP factor.

TARP did not create prosperity. Only a free, prosperous economy can do that, not the government.

Lie #2 All business owners are greedy rich people.

Anyone who goes into business does it to make money. The average self-employed American's family has five times the net worth of the average wage earners. The payoff can be high if you succeed. Only one big problem: success is difficult to achieve.

When you start your own business, everything depends on you. It requires money, time, materials, production, and labor to make it happen along with your total commitment, and no guarantee of success.

The U.S. Bureau of labor Statistics claims, one third of all businesses fail in two years. More than half have gone by four years. It does not matter what type of business; they all follow these scary statistics.

You can become well off financially running your own business. It will not happen fast if it happens at all. Those who have never owned a business are quick to point out the wealth business owners appear to have. What they don't look at is the constant, unending risk and ever-increasing expenses of being in business.

Imagine opening a store. Before it opens, the owner has to buy or rent the building, buy all the goods to be sold, hire and pay employees, pay for heat, electricity and water, pay for local and state government licenses; all before anyone pays him a penny. He prays people will buy his goods or services, or else.

Lie #3, a college education insures a higher income.

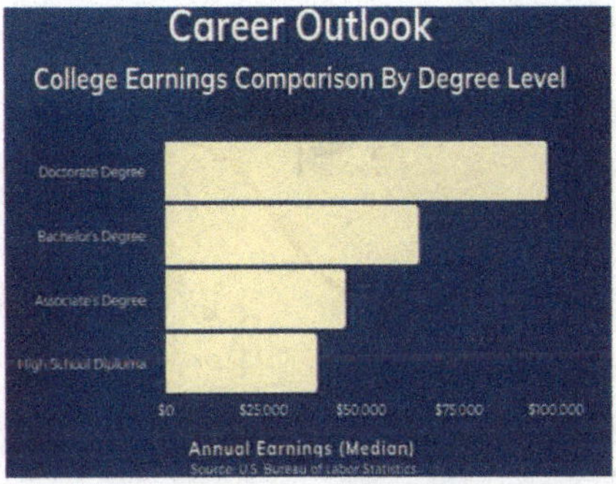

The chart shows why parents push their kids to get as much education as possible. Parents want the best for their kids. Success in America is judged too often by income level.

It is fun to point out that of the twenty current richest people in the world, seven dropped out of High School or college. Another seven do not give their education because it's embarrassing. The rest have degrees as follows: one Associate, two bachelor and three masters.

For some brilliant people, education gets in the way of their creativity and making money. The work we get is based on what we know, the more you know the more you will be able to do. Whatever you do, don't be a dummy, learn something somehow. Remember being educated does not always mean college.

Consider the education level of private business owners. These are among the most prosperous in the country. These are the people who drive employment. Most have a moderate level of education; few have a college degree.

The last consideration is the cost of education in modern America. In the past several years the cost of education has skyrocketed.

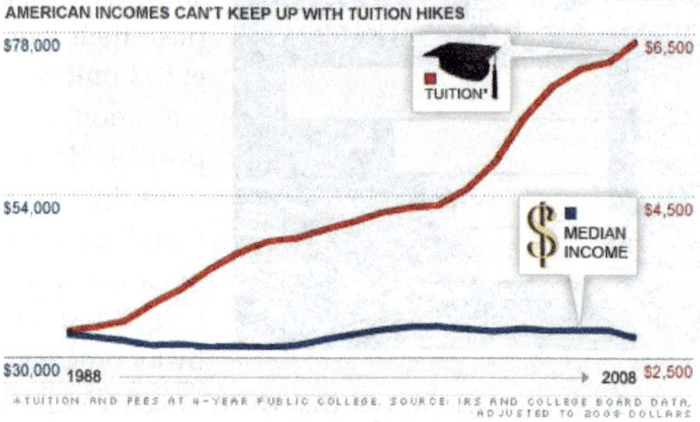

The dramatic increases in college tuition have been accompanied by growing federal higher education loans, a 90% bump in the past ten years. Universities are encouraged to raise prices because federal loans allow students to easily take the debt. Students are less likely to object to the rising prices since they are not spending their own money. This has created a debt-ridden graduating class each year.

These grads march into a shrinking marketplace where employment is scarce. The advantage of making several thousand a year more is cancelled by the payment schedules for education loans.

In the 1970s, 12% of young people were college graduates. Today, over 25% of young adults obtain a degree. The proliferation of degrees has lessened their value. More employers want degreed people for less significant, lower paying positions.

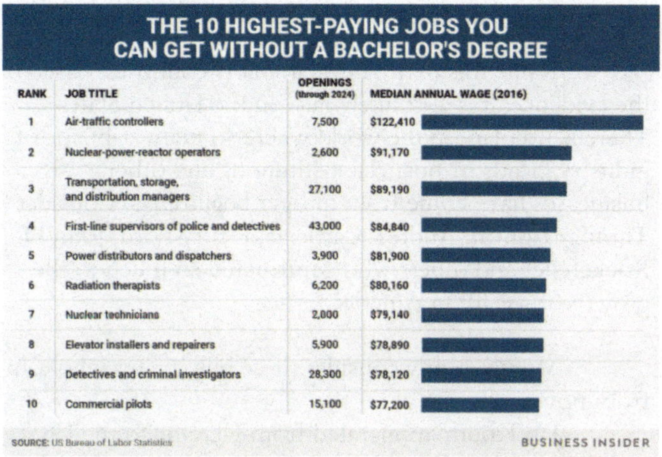

THE 10 HIGHEST-PAYING JOBS YOU CAN GET WITHOUT A BACHELOR'S DEGREE

RANK	JOB TITLE	OPENINGS (through 2024)	MEDIAN ANNUAL WAGE (2016)
1	Air-traffic controllers	7,500	$122,410
2	Nuclear-power-reactor operators	2,600	$91,170
3	Transportation, storage, and distribution managers	27,100	$89,190
4	First-line supervisors of police and detectives	43,000	$84,840
5	Power distributors and dispatchers	3,900	$81,900
6	Radiation therapists	6,200	$80,160
7	Nuclear technicians	2,800	$79,140
8	Elevator installers and repairers	5,900	$78,890
9	Detectives and criminal investigators	28,300	$78,120
10	Commercial pilots	15,100	$77,200

SOURCE: US Bureau of Labor Statistics — BUSINESS INSIDER

Employers are savvy people. They look for candidates who know who they are and what they want.

Lie #4, it is difficult for the poor to become rich.

While this may be true in many countries, based on the evidence, it is absolutely false in the United States. There is no place in the world where so many captains of industry, heads of financial institutions and other businesses have come from meager beginnings. Consider Thomas Edison, Andrew Carneige, Henry Ford, John D. Rockefeller and others who contributed so much to the growth of wealth in America.

More recently consider these billionaires who came from poverty.

Jan Koum immigrated from Ukraine to the US with his mother. Although they lived on food stamps, he taught himself coding and later founded WhatsApp. Koum sold WhatsApp to Facebook for $19 billion.

Jeff Bezos was the son of a teenage mother who later got adopted by his Cuban immigrant stepfather, Jeff Bezos, excelled in school. In 1994, he quit a Wall Street job to start an online bookstore in his garage. That startup, Amazon, grew into the world's most dominant e-commerce empire.

Do Won Chang who came from South Korea with little money, worked as a janitor and a gas station clerk to survive. He had a dream and was determined to make it happen. He and his wife later founded Forever 21 and turned his shop into a global fast-fashion empire.

Howard Schultz grew up in a poor Brooklyn housing complex; After joining a small Seattle coffee chain, he reimagined it as a cultural institution. Under his leadership, Starbucks transformed from a local roastery into a worldwide coffee powerhouse.

In a free market system, people have unlimited opportunities to change their fortune.

Lie #5, public programs provide money and jobs.

Public works projects are said to create jobs and circulate more money. They do this at the expense of the taxpayer. If the theory of sending a little money to the government improves the economy, then would it not also be true that sending most of our income would improve it more.

The truth is that money not sent to the government always stimulates an economy. Earners spend more, creating more jobs when they have more to spend. The jobs the government provides cause private businesses to compete for employees with the government. The resulting higher wages cause higher prices.

Government programs that advocate the increase in jobs and money ignore where the money comes from. Governments produce nothing. Building a dam or road may benefit business eventually if we overlook the fact that the funds to build the bridge, road, or dam, are forcibly taken from the businesses it purports to help. The only source of money is the marketplace, unless you discover a gold mine. Even there you are going to work.

The idea that a government pays for anything flies in the face of the SAP factor. None of us would be stupid enough to give our money to our friend Bill to build a bridge, road, or dam, and then say it cost us nothing. Yet the government does just that all the time. The truth is we all pay for public programs.

Lie #6, open immigration improves the economy.

There is a prevailing theory that the influx of immigrants, legal and illegal are a benefit to American economy. There are absolutely no statistics to support such a claim. Certainly, there are people who come to this country and become well employed, or start businesses, thereby contributing to the economy. There are others who come here and do no more than go on the roles of welfare programs. To declare that these millions of illegals are a benefit is preposterous.

In 2025, ICE spent $3.2 billion to identify, arrest, detain, and remove half a million undocumented immigrants, according to the Department of Homeland Security. ICE is interested in the worst of the illegals: criminals, and other dangerous types. It would take thousands of commercial flights to remove most of the 11 million illegal immigrants. None of this is a benefit to the country's economy, it is an economic nightmare.

In the late 19th and early 20th century immigration was carefully controlled, limiting those entering the country to those healthy and those potentially beneficial. Modern transportation has changed that, along with a failure to control the borders.

Six states have almost two thirds of all unauthorized immigrants: California, Texas, Florida, New York, New Jersey and Illinois. Many of these have lived here for a decade or more. About eight million of these people are thought to be gainfully employed.

The cost of border control is huge. Over the past 24 years, the number of border patrol agents has increased 500 percent; the amount of border wall has grown from 77 miles to 700 miles.

Lie #7, tariffs protect local industries.

Eliminating tariffs on foreign goods would allow people to buy products more cheaply, leaving them more money to buy American products, and encourage foreign countries to buy more in this country.

In *The Wealth of Nations*, Adam Smith said,

> *"In every country it is and always must be the interest of the great body of the people to buy whatever they want of those who sell it the cheapest."*

Tariffs set a false economy that reduces prosperity. Foreign cars sold in the US have forced both the production of better and cheaper vehicles through competition. It also increased the amount of foreign investment in American production plants. While individual companies have suffered, the country has economically benefited and increased foreign markets for American vehicles.

In a recent study, for every 10% rise in Chinese imports in a given industry, there was a 3% increase in legal work, a 4% increase in IT requirements, and a 12% increase in research and development. While competition is eating the one end of the market, it's providing additional work at the other end. As a nation, we should be accepting this challenge and fighting to innovate more and shift more of our workforce to knowledge work.

When the consumer spends less per item, he usually buys more stuff, increasing domestic purchasing.

Lie #8, the minimum wage helps the poor.

Politicians say minimum wages make sure everyone gets livable pay. Hiring employees comes at a price. In the case of labor that price is called a wage, which has an unusual concept added to it that does not belong to other prices. The concept that wages should support the person getting them. No other price has such an attachment.

When a price minimum is set by the government, it has immediate adverse effects. The first is that businesses will not hire anyone who is worth less than the minimum. This typically affects those at the bottom of the economic ladder most.

The second effect is tied to the pricing of products. Industries able to pay the additional cost of minimum wages will pass that cost on to their customers. That rise in prices hits the poorest class the hardest. Industries unable to raise their prices adjust in other ways to meet the law and keep their income positive. This often means labor reduction of some type, or moving the business offshore, or closing operations.

None of this benefits the poor.

Large corporations are not disturbed by such a price law, few of their employees fall into the lowest pay range. Small, new and marginal businesses are hurt. Often these are enterprises owned by the poorer class. Private companies, the heart of American business, must make the most adjustment. As always, the SAP factor rules, and business has only one source of income, the customer.

If the pay for a McDonald worker is $15.00 per hour, the cost of the hamburgers must double, or the workforce must be cut in half. The food service industry being the biggest employer of minimum wage workers.

If the minimum wage laws help the poor, then it should be clear that more and better jobs are provided by the enactment of these laws. The opposite is true; the minimum wage laws have made the situation for these people worse.

Take the case of teenage blacks. Before the passing and increase in the minimum wage, back in the 1940s, black teenage unemployment figures were lower than white teenage unemployment. In fact, black teenage unemployment was lower in 1948 and 49, a time of economic recession, than at any time since, even with ever increasing minimum wage amounts.

FIGURE 2

Employment to population ratio

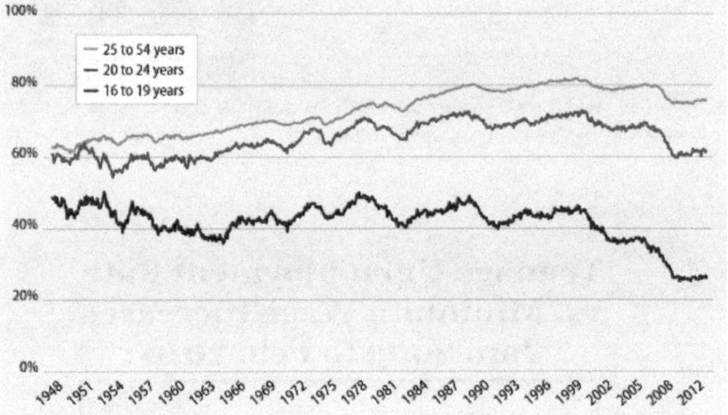

Source: Bureau of Labor Statistics.

The above chart shows employment rates since 1948. Notice that the greatest decline in employment has been among teenagers. 50% fewer teenagers are employed today compared to before the increases in pay by minimum wage laws.

In the chart below, it can be seen by the government's own estimation that employment decreases as the minimum wage increases.

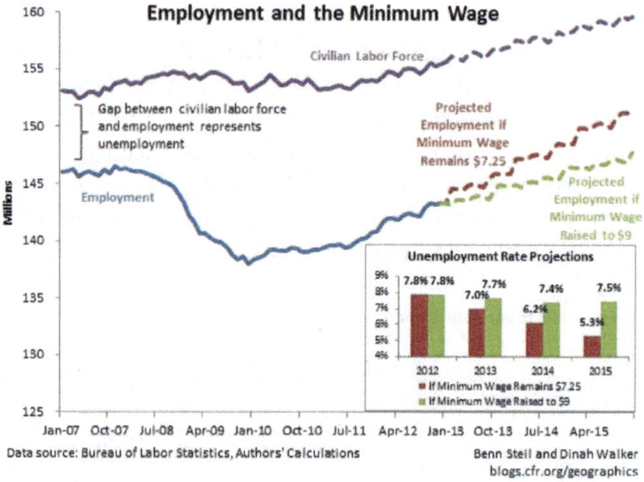

Lie #9, technology and efficiency eliminate jobs.

When computer technology grew in the 1970s it was thought that it would eliminate millions of jobs along with all paperwork. The following three decades proved to do precisely the opposite with both paper and labor.

The union at General Motors wanted to prevent the use of the paint roller two decades earlier. It was presumed to eliminate jobs. Its use did no such thing, though much more painting was done far faster.

There are many more examples tied to the idiotic assumption that life has a limited amount of work. The correct principle is that work increases because of technology and efficiency.

The same people who fear the changes brought on by technical improvements understand that modern society grew from the cross pollination of the grasses to create wheat. Wheat needed to make bread, the staple of civilization, must be developed, it does not occur in nature. Once men understood this, a few men could farm wheat to sustain many. Many did not sit on their haunches; they made other products and services with the time they gained as a result of being released from gathering food. It is silly to worry that if some work is eliminated no other work can be found. Technology, which created additional jobs in the beginning, creates more, not less, as it frees people to do other work.

While it is true that the automobile put many carriage makers and blacksmiths out of work, it created millions of new jobs while increasing the wealth of many more. Neither did the horse disappear though its use changed, which frankly was better for both horse and man.

Lie #10, social welfare helps the poor.

Since the 1960s Americans have supported ever bigger and more generous government welfare programs. The "Great Society" of President Johnson declared that we were wealthy enough to support our poor.

America's welfare state is an empire bigger than the entire budgets of almost every other country in the world. There are 184 federal welfare programs, most jointly financed and administered by the states. Food Stamps, also called the Bridge Card, went to 47 million Americans in 2012. There is also the Special Supplemental Nutrition Program for Women, Infants and Children. There is a School Breakfast Program and School Lunch Program. There is the Summer Food Service Program for Children. There are Child and Adult Care Food Programs, the Emergency Food Assistance Program, and the Commodity Supplemental Food Program. A Nutrition Program for the Elderly. Federal spending for Food and Nutrition Assistance overall has climbed to over $100 billion a year.

Next, is federal housing assistance. This includes expenditures for over 1 million public housing units owned by the government. It includes Section 8 rental assistance for nearly another 4 million private housing units. Then there is Rural Rental Assistance, Rural Housing Loans, and Rural Rental Housing Loans. Also, included is Home Investment Partnerships, Community Development Block Grants, and Housing for Special Populations, Housing Opportunities for Persons with AIDS, Emergency Shelter Grants, the Supportive Housing program, the Single Room Occupancy program, the Shelter Plus Care program, and the Home Ownership and Opportunity for People Everywhere program.

There is the Earned Income Tax Credit, which sends low-income workers checks even though they usually pay no taxes. The Child Tax Credit similarly provides cash to families with children. Supplemental Security Income provides cash for the low income aged, blind and disabled.

CHART 2

Total Means-Tested Welfare Spending and Official Poverty Rate, 1947–2012

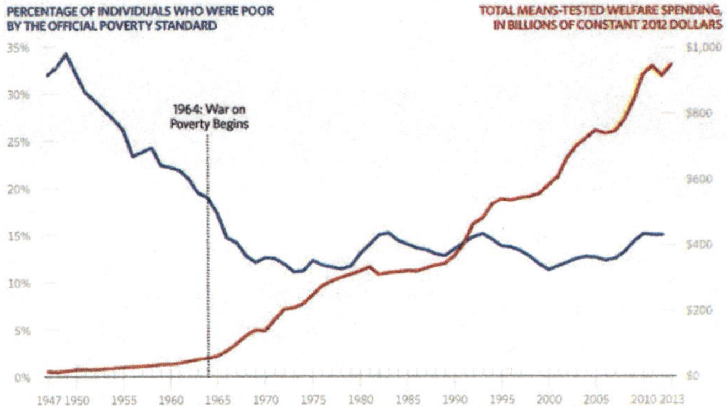

Sources: Poverty figures for 1947-1958: Gordon Fisher, "Estimates of the Poverty Population Under the Current Official Definition for Years Before 1959," U.S. Department of Health and Human Services, Office of the Assistant Secretary for Planning and Evaluation, 1986. Poverty figures for 1959-2012: U.S. Census Bureau, Current Population Survey, Annual Social and Economic Supplements, "Historical Poverty Tables—People," Table 2, https://www.census.gov/hhes/www/poverty/data/historical/people.html (accessed September 10, 2014). Means-tested welfare spending figures: Heritage Foundation research, U.S. Office of Management and Budget.

BG 2955 heritage.org

The federal government also provides the Social Services Block Grant, the Community Services Block Grant, and the Legal Services Corporation, to the needy.

Based on the size of this expenditure one might hope for a big decline in poverty. Yet the rate that was at 14% in the 1960s has remained unchanged for decades. Trillions of dollars have done nothing to erase poverty

Cryptocurrency

A cryptocurrency is a computerized technology currency. It is also called digital currency. There are no coins or paper version. The photo above is only a logo for Bitcoin, a cryptocurrency that is only found on a computer. Bitcoin does not mint any physical coins or print any certificates.

Because it works through a computer network, cryptocurrency is not dependent on any central authority, such as a government or bank, to give it value or maintain it. Individual coin ownership records are stored in a digital ledger or blockchain.

A **blockchain** is a computer database or ledger that stores records in a network of computers. The information is transparent, unchangeable, and resistant to tampering. Each "block" contains data, and the blocks are linked in a chronological chain. All users on the chain may see all the activity and make transactions, but no one has control. Blockchain is best known for its role in cryptocurrency systems but are not limited to cryptocurrency uses. Blockchains can be used to make data in any industry immutable, meaning it cannot be altered.

Bitcoin was created in 2009. Since then, blockchain use has exploded due to the creation of dozens of cryptocurrencies. Bitcoin is one of a large number of cryptocurrencies, such as Ethereum, Steller Lumins, Tether and Solana, that can be purchased through leading crypto exchanges found online.

In a blockchain transaction information is entered into a 4MB file called a **block**. Different blockchains have different-sized blocks. Once the block is full, the block data is run through a cryptographic hash function, which creates a hexadecimal number called the **block header hash**. The hash is then entered into encrypted form with the other information connecting to other blocks, creating a chain of blocks, or "blockchain."

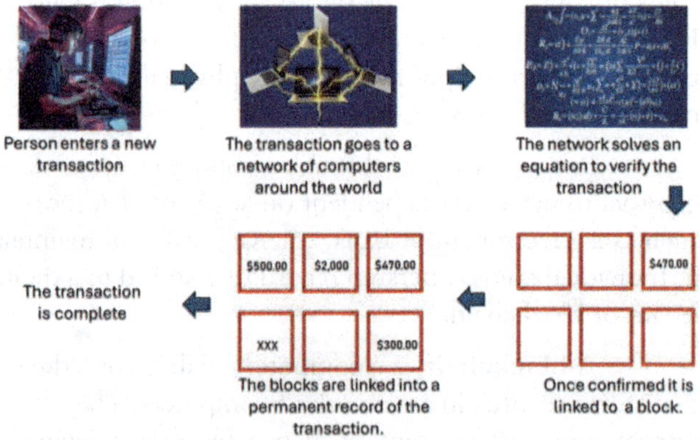

Since cryptocurrency is not controlled by any government or bank it cannot be taxed. Nor can the transactions be taxed. Nor can the increase in value be taxed. Governments cannot either detect or interfere with cryptocurrency transactions. Governments do not like this feature of cryptocurrency. Unless the cryptocurrency is converted to dollars the government is powerless to tax it.

Bitcoin, the first decentralized cryptocurrency, was launched in 2009 by Satoshi Nakamoto with the mining of the first block. The first real-world transaction took place

in 2010 when 10,000 Bitcoin were used to buy two pizzas. At that point it was not valued above $4.00.

The value of only one Bitcoin reached $126,000.00 in October of 2025, its highest value so far. In early 2026 the dollar value of one Bitcoin was reduced to $75,000.00.

That kind of value increase attracted the notice of big investors and banks. These institutional financial firms started buying digital currency. This action took Bitcoin from simply being a **medium of exchange** to being a **store of value** too.

Let's look at those terms. A **medium of exchange** means something of value that can function in an economic transaction between two parties.

A **store of value** means that something of value can be held for a period of time and keeps or increases its value. By being both a medium of exchange and a store of value Bitcoin qualifies as **money**. It's just not government money.

With all the cryptocurrencies on the market, it's important to understand the different types. Knowing whether the coin has a purpose can help in planning whether it is worth an investment. A cryptocurrency with a purpose is less risky than one that doesn't have a use.

Coin names differ from coin types. Here are some of the types you'll find, with some of the names of tokens in that category:

- **Utility**: XRP and ETH are two examples of utility tokens. They serve specific functions on their respective blockchains.

- **Transactional**: Tokens designed to be used as a payment method. Bitcoin is the most well-known of these.
- **Governance**: These tokens represent voting or other rights on a blockchain, such as Uniswap.6
- **Platform**: These tokens support decentralized applications, which are built on a blockchain, such as Solana.7
- **Security tokens or asset-backed tokens**: Tokens representing ownership of an asset, such as a tokenized stock value transferred to the blockchain. MS Token is an example of a securitized token.

To buy cryptocurrency you will need to visit a cryptocurrency exchange. These are businesses that allow you to buy or sell cryptocurrencies from other users at the current market price. After buying the coins, you will need to transfer them to a crypto wallet or use a third-party service like Coinbase to store your coins. Coinbase sells and stores coins.

To buy cryptocurrency as an investment, you may be able to do so through your online brokerage. Robinhood, is also a top broker for cryptocurrency trading, allows users to invest in Bitcoin and other cryptocurrencies. Several crypto ETFs, such as Spot Bitcoin and Ethereum ETFs, allow investment in crypto without having to maintain their wallets. ETFs are **exchange-traded funds** that offer exposure to crypto price movements. The SEC initially blocked ETFs that directly held bitcoin before approving them in 2024. Investors may choose to hold Bitcoin ETF shares or Ether spot shares, which the SEC approved.

In 2024 the launch of the first Bitcoin and Ethereum ETFs, indicated genuine financial institution adoption. President Trump's support for Bitcoin added to its credibility. This makes cryptocurrency's future more positive. The Trump administration wants to establish a Strategic Bitcoin Reserve (SBR) for the United States. While adding Bitcoin to the U.S. Treasury's balance sheet would require congressional approval, the mere suggestion is positive for cryptocurrency. The stage is being set for widespread acceptance and use of Cryptocurrency.

Progress and Progressivism

Theodore Roosevelt

The **Progressive Movement** began in earnest with President Theodore Roosevelt.

Progressives wanted to cure the ills of American society that had developed during the industrial growth in the latter portion of the 19th century. The frontier had become part of the business community, great cities and businesses flourished.

The progressive reform, following the abolition of slavery, began during Reconstruction and lasted until the 1920s. The struggle for women's rights, the temperance movement, and the progressive income tax were some of the issues addressed.

A farm aid movement also emerged to compensate for the decline of rural America as masses of Americans moved from the country to the city. This movement occurred because of the higher wages and easier life in industry, and the dramatic increase in mechanized farm productivity that required much less labor. All of this brought massive changes to the American economy.

Progressivism was rooted in the belief that man's intellect could solve all the problems of society.

Progressivism was the attempt to regulate sectors of the economy and redistribute wealth and private property. These policies, many progressives argued, would not be enacted as long as the political process was dominated by powerful special interests and the Constitution that blocked their desired actions.

Specific goals included: ending corruption and the influence powerful men had on government, the effort to include people more directly in the political process, and the conviction that government must solve social problems.

Progressives wanted to establish **fairness** in society called **'social justice'**. They went beyond wanting simply equal opportunity for all to guarantee total equality in every possible way.

The single notable exception to this generous attitude concerned black Americans. Progressives had no interest in improving the opportunity or situation of blacks.

The success of progressivism owed much to publicity generated by the muckrakers, writers who detailed the horrors of poverty, urban slums, dangerous factory conditions, and child labor, among a host of other ills. Upton Sinclair and Charles Edward Russell were among the muckrakers. These writers supported a combination of advertising, boycotts, dirty tricks and phony patriotism, used by progressives to obtain their aims.

The attacks extended to criticism of "unfair" business practices, of monopolies, trusts, and the political influence of the rich. The writing of muckrakers prevailed even though shown to be based on false claims under later investigation.

The cry for "social justice" was created to pit the rich against the poor. It is hard to separate the idea of the oppressors against the oppressed of the progressives from that used by the communists. The progressive philosophy accused the rich of gaining wealth only from exploitation of poorer people. This is Marxist thought dressed in less intimidating clothes. It reduces the situation of the lower classes to that of a helpless victim from which only the power of government can rescue them. It denies the power of personal achievement in the face of the fact that all the wealthy men of this "Gilded Age" came from desperately poor families.

Progressives believed the economic elites enjoy greater wealth, and therefore influence, than the ordinary citizen, and they exploit these advantages politically, using them as leverage to obtain still greater wealth and influence. Since the desire for wealth and power is rarely satisfied, there tend to be recurring cycles of concentrated political and economic power, together with corruption.

In truth, the success of the biggest industries of the early 20th century have been proven repeatedly to have gained their position from efficiency and lower prices. If people were taken advantage of by these industries why did wages and consumer purchasing rise so dramatically during that period?

The Progressive Era would not have had powerful influence had it not been for the Constitutional amendment process. The 16th, 17th, 18th and 19th amendments reworked the constitution expanding the power of the federal government, one of the main goals of progressives.

The 16th Amendment was the key to government power. It authorized Congress, against the original intent of the founding fathers, to take the property of citizens, especially the property of the richest citizens. Theodore Roosevelt, who used federal power to take over private business, said during the 1902 coal strike, "To hell with the Constitution when people want coal!"

The progressive creation of the Federal Reserve, never authorized by the constitution or its amendments, completed federal control of the American money system.

After Roosevelt and Taft, President Woodrow Wilson sought to overcome the constitution's separation

of powers. He thought that a more powerful presidency would create a more aggressive federal government that the progressive agenda required. He is responsible for giving the federal government control of issues of money and banking by the creation, in 1913, of the **Federal Reserve** that to this day dominates our financial condition.

Wilson ended the long battles over what are called business trusts: groups of companies with control of a market. The Clayton Trust Act of 1914 put the government in charge of the way companies compete.

Americans rejected the work of progressives by electing Calvin Coolidge President in 1923. He reduced the income tax on all Americans, especially the rich, who had been paying 70% of income. Curiously, the federal government collected more taxes at lower rates. That is because people and business have more money to spend, and the dollar is taxed each time it is spent.

The result was the roaring 20s, a time of unprecedented growth in American individual wealth. Many working Americans were buying stock. For the first time, more Americans lived in cities than on farms. The nation's total wealth more than doubled, creating a consumer society that bought radios, ice boxes, private homes, automobiles, and clothing at an unprecedented rate. America partied hard with families experiencing more free time than ever before in history.

The Federal Reserve System worked feverishly to maintain the artificial rate of exchange of the U.S. Dollar by restricting the domestic money supply, this caused the collapse of banks after the stock market crash in 1929 and caused the great depression.

The **New Deal** of President Franklin D. Roosevelt **resurrected the progressive era.** His efforts extended and deepened the depression by vastly expanding the size and power of the federal government. His **National Labor Relations Act** strengthened collective bargaining, and the **Works Progress Administration** generated thousands of jobs building major construction projects, still it made no dent in the depression. Social security, passed in 1933, giving the single biggest boost to federal income ever.

Most of his legislation was found unconstitutional by the Supreme Court. Roosevelt then asked Congress to expand the number of Supreme Court justices so he could appoint justices sympathetic to his cause without regard for constitutional law. He forcefully demanded six new judges on the Supreme Court and up to 44 additional lower Federal judgeships.

In 1939, Roosevelt established the EOP, **Executive Office of the President,** designed to find ways to get around the pesky U.S. Constitution. Many of Roosevelt's executive orders were indifferent to civil liberties and democratic values; the worst occurred after the Japanese bombing of Pearl Harbor. FDR authorized the internment of thousands of American citizens in concentration camps because they happened to be of Japanese descent.

Under the administration of Lyndon B. Johnson, a progressive president, the **Great Society** emerged in 1964. Johnson claimed we had the money and the obligation to support the poor of America. From the Great Society, the government created the "entitlement programs" that proceed from one year to another with an unlimited budget, as if America will never run short of money. President Johnson also declared a War on Poverty.

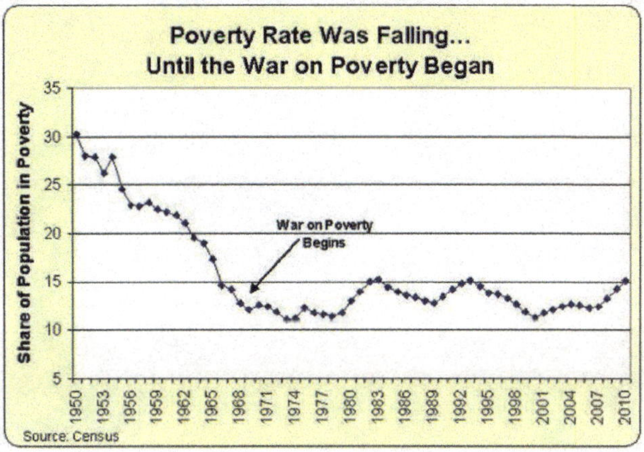

The modern 'nanny state' is rooted in Progressive legislation. Income tax and social security confiscate the wealth of productive Americans, and the Fed continues to inflate the dollar. All the work of the progressive movement.

How to Become a Slave

"The rich rule over the poor, and the borrower is servant to the lender." Proverbs 22:7

Do not suppose that slavery has gone out of fashion. There are plenty who sign up for slavery each year. Not in some far foreign country run by scoundrels, but right here in the United States of America. They actually sign an agreement. In the days of legal servitude in early America, people signed agreements to work for someone for a number of years. In the end, they would gain freedom and a new start in life. These days, people sign agreements to pay for cars, houses, vacations and the almighty credit card. This is slavery too.

Want some really big debt, go to college. The average college graduate has $27,000.00 in debt. This means that a person of the same age who did not go to college for four years, who worked, avoided debt and saved, is $100,000 ahead in the lifetime income game.

Also, as said previously, if he avoided debt, he is servant to no one.

Debt for education, an automobile, and a home are considered by many Americans to be not only normal, but necessary. The concept stems from the need to get an education to get a good job, and a car to get to work.

Nobody ever says that one needs to have $40,000.00 in debt to get started in life. Yet, the total debt for a car and a college education easily amounts to this handsome figure. The debtor is obliged to two creditors. These creditors have the right to demand payment on schedule. The debtor, in turn, is servant to the creditors and the schedules. The work the debtor does to earn money is not for himself alone. The work must first serve the creditors.

The guy who did not go to college, who also has paid cash for his car, may use all his income, except taxes, for himself. This means that the guy with no debt can save more against future needs, for which he will have cash to meet those needs. Alas, the poor educated fellow must borrow more money to meet his future needs, since his extra money is going to his creditors. The cycle for the debtor leads to more debt.

The same situation for the debt free person leads to greater financial power. The debtor becomes ever more a slave, the debt free, ever stronger and more independent.

If you have heard the common proverb, "the rich get richer and the poor get poorer," this may be what it means. Christ said, "To he that has it shall be given, and to he that has not it shall be taken away, even that which he has." Matthew 13:12

On top of the looming shadow described by the debtor there is a more sinister time lurking. The poor man gets laid off, fired, or his job is terminated, along with the income that paid his debts and basic needs. Without work he can neither feed his needs nor pay his creditors. The debt free fellow, devastated with the same circumstances, resorts to using his savings temporarily, he has no creditors to satisfy.

If our debtor does not find a way to make the car payments the repo man will take it from him. If he cannot make his unsecured loan, he might go bankrupt, except the government will not dismiss education loans under the bankruptcy law. Talk about your indentured slavery, this is as inescapable as slavery. If our debtor owns a house he may protect it under bankruptcy law, but he will still have to fulfill the mortgage payments. It is possible at this point to see the implied chains and manacles fastened to the debtor. When he finds a job, he will find it extremely difficult to borrow any more money, because of damage to his credit record. The downward spiral resists a reversal as much as locked irons to the ankles.

In all of this we have never mentioned, excuse my language, the credit card. Holy charge account Batman, everybody must have a credit card! Not so grasshopper, and here is why. Credit card debt is expensive. Unpaid balances carry monthly interest rates near 25 percent. Carrying an unpaid balance from month to month means paying a monthly premium charge.

A $2,000 balance on a credit card, on which only the monthly minimum is paid, will take thirty-two years to pay off. The total amount paid, including interest, will be $10,000; a high price for $2,000 worth of stuff.

The multi-billion-dollar credit card industry wants everyone to have a credit card. The losses they take for non-payment are worth it. Think about what they do. They manufacture nothing. They ship nothing. They don't hire huge workforces. They pay bills for card holders, then charge them the highest percentage fee in lending for doing it.

They also charge the sellers of goods and services for the privilege of processing the card at their business. The sellers are happy to pay the fee, knowing that a card holder will, on average, spend 33% more than a cash customer. When McDonald's decided to accept credit cards, sales to card customers jumped almost 50% above what cash customers pay.

It is easy to see the psychology is different for credit cards and cash payments. Face it, the cash customers

see their dollars leave their wallet. They know the purchase resulted in a loss of money. The credit card customer uses the card and puts it back in their wallet; it appears to have been at no loss. They know they will get a bill at the end of the month, but they get a bill at the end of every month anyhow. The guy who pays cash is done at the point of purchase.

There is no upside to credit cards. Even those who try to pay off the card every month still face additional charges. The credit card companies love to hide charges in the timing of the payment versus the time of the charge.

Few people do pay the entire bill each month. The Banking Association says the average American family carries a $10,000 balance on a variety of credit cards. What a good deal for credit card companies. They make $2.5

billion a year in interest from just one million customers. What we learn from this is that it is a good idea to run a credit card company; it is bad to use credit cards. Consider this question: how many of your friends would be willing to borrow money from you at 25% interest? Doesn't that rate make you sound like a loan shark?

There are rebates, paybacks, and free air miles with credit cards. Take the SAP factor into consideration on these. The only reason they give out anything is because it is paid for by someone. The only source they have for their income is card holders. In the end, the card holder only gets back what he has already paid. The card represents nothing more than the card holder's manacles.

The best example of saving over borrowing:

If you have not heard your parents or other grown-ups, say it, just ask to see if they tell you, "You will always have to make a car payment".

Who, pray tell, is the demon that came up with that rule? Is it a government mandate on the public? Is it taught in public school?

"It ain't true."

No one is required to be in debt. You can choose to be debt free, own a car, and never make a payment. Which is good news, since it is tough to do anything without a car. This does not mean you have to suffer either.

Consider a new car, if you get a good deal, costs $25.000 to $30,000, and is devalued down to $20,000 to $24,000 as soon as it leaves the dealership. Try and sell a brand-new car with no mileage and see what you get. The poor fellow who drives the new car pays $300 to $450 a month, in six years he will pay over $30,000 on his $25,000 loan, at which point the car is worth about $6,000.

Suppose instead, you scrape up $1,500 to $2,000 and gets a descent "clunker" to drive for one year. During that one-year period, you put $300 to $450 in a saving account each month. In a year, you will have $3,600 to $5,400 to spend on a newer car plus $1,500 for the clunker or $5,100 to $6,900. Quite a step up. Since you paid cash again, there are still no payments.

It works so well; you keep saving at that rate of $5,000 a year, which moves you to a $12,000 car for cash the next year. You buy an $18,000 car the following year. Check it out, you are up to an $18,000 car in three years. You can go on never making a car payment or suffer the losses attached to borrowing. You can do this and buy car every year. Unlike your neighbor you can skip a savings payment any time you want.

Being a smart person, a saver never buys a new car even after hitting the $24,000 level in two more years. The loss of value of any vehicle that first year is just too high. Never lease either. Leasing is the most expensive way to have a car.

Suppose instead of a monthly car payment $100.00 was invested in a mutual fund. At a 10% return on investment. That investment would earn about $20,775,20 in 10 years; it would make $76,669.69 in twenty years, and at thirty years $228,023.53. Not a bad return for a small monthly payment.

A Final Word

"A democracy is always temporary in nature; it simply cannot exist as a permanent form of government. A democracy will continue to exist up until the time that voters discover they can vote themselves generous gifts from the public treasury. From that moment on, the majority always votes for the candidates who promise the most benefits from the public treasury, with the result that every democracy will finally collapse due to loose fiscal policy, which is always followed by a dictatorship. The average age of the world's greatest civilizations from the beginning of history, has been about 200 years. During those 200 years, these nations always progressed through the following sequence:

1. From bondage to spiritual faith;
2. From spiritual faith to great courage;
3. From courage to liberty;
4. From liberty to abundance;
5. From abundance to complacency;
6. From complacency to apathy;
7. From apathy to dependence;
8. From dependence back into bondage "

Alexander Tyler 1787

Vocabulary of Economic Terms

16th Amendment – Allowed the income tax.

Bankruptcy – the absolute inability to pay debt.

Bonds – May be Government, public or private papers promising to pay a specific amount to the holder for an investment.

Boom – A strong upward thrust of an economy in which demand is high.

Bretton Woods - system of monetary management established the rules for commercial and financial relations among the world's major industrial states in the mid-20th century.

Budget – A list of payments and income showing the gain or loss, over time, for a given entity.

Budget Process – A long detailed process in which congress and its bureaucratic financial departments determine how much money will be spent each year.

Business climate – The relative strength or weakness on an economy.

Civil Law - The law of ancient Rome as embodied in the Justinian code, especially that which applied to private citizens.

Communist – A society in which all goods are shared according to need in the absence of property ownership

Communist Manifesto– Karl Marx and Friedrisch Engles book on communist philosophy.

Demand – The amount of a product or service wanted by buyers in a given period of time.

Deutschmark Mark – The official monetary unit of the German people prior to the Euro dollar.

Enfranchisement - to grant a franchise to; admit to citizenship, especially to the right of voting.

Entitlements – Government promises to pay individuals for certain named conditions.

Federal Reserve – The Federal Reserve System or "Fed", is an agency of congress allowed to print money and set interest rates.

Fiat currencies - Currency that a government has declared to be legal tender, even though it has no intrinsic value and is not backed by reserves

Free Markets – A state in which business operates without undue restriction from authority.

French Franc – The official monetary Unit of France prior to the Euro dollar.

GDP – The Gross Domestic Product, usually per year, of a given country or state, showing the sum of all its production in that year in units of money.

Inflation - substantial rise in the general level of prices related to an increase in the volume of money and resulting in the loss of value of currency

Laissez-faire – the absence of government interference in the workings of the free market.

Market - where buyers and the sellers of goods or services have potential for a transaction to take place.

Macroeconomics – The study of financial variations dealing with large economic entities.

Microeconomics – The study of financial variations dealing with small, usually individual or business economic entities.

Minimum wage – A law forcing employers to pay a certain hourly rate.

Mortgage – The borrowing of money against real property assets, like a house or building, for the purpose of taking possession and eventual ownership.

Natural Law - A law or body of laws that derives from nature and is believed to be binding upon human actions apart from or in conjunction with laws established by human authority.

Non-profit business – A business operating not for the purpose of making a profit.

Pound Sterling - the official name for the standard monetary unit of the United Kingdom

Private business – A business operated and owned by an individual or individuals.

Profit - A financial benefit realized when the amount of revenue gained from a business activity exceeds the expenses, costs and taxes needed to sustain the activity. Any profit that is gained goes to the business's owners, who may or may not decide to spend it on the business.

Public Business – A business that sells company stock to the public.

Risk – Chance taking in which money, property and labor are exposed to loss in order to achieve a given goal.

ROI Return on Investment, or the amount of money gained or lost after invested in an entity.

Roman Currency – Official monetary units of the Roman Empire.

Rule of 72 – A way of determining when an investment will double.

Smith Dictum - Each person seeking their own self-interest results in what is best for everyone.

Social equality - An ideal condition in which all members of a society have the same rights, security, opportunities, obligations and **social** benefits.

Socialism – A society in which goods and money of all are pooled for equal benefit.

Stimulate economy – A process in which an economy grows as a result of a particular activity by government or other entity.

Stock Market Crash – An event in which a stock market has prices fall so low it is unable to operate.

Stocks – Papers of public ownership in a business that gain or lose value with the fortunes of the company.

Tariffs - A list or system of duties imposed by a government on imported or exported goods.

TARP - The $700 billion *Troubled Asset Relief Program* of the United States government to purchase assets and equity from financial institutions to strengthen its financial sector.

Tax rate – The percentage of tax charges against a person or business.

Troy weight - A system of weights and measures in which the grain is the same as in the avoirdupois system, and a pound contains 12 ounces, or 5,760 grains. Troy weight is used primarily by miners and gold dealers.

Venture Capital – Money put forth in a new business with the hope of increased value.

Sources

A series of articles by Walter E. Williams
"Drugs, Economics, and liberty," Ideas on Liberty, (June 2010).

"Washington's Lies," Ideas on Liberty, (October 2010).

"Government and Conflict," Ideas on Liberty, (January/February 2011).

"Poverty is Easy to Explain," Ideas on Liberty, (May 2011).

"Forked-tongued Washington Government," Ideas on Liberty, (September 2011).

"Population Control Nonsense," Ideas on Liberty, (December 2011).

Also go the Walter E. Williams web site: www.econ.gmu/edu/web

"*Power of the Market*" Milton Friedman a series of brief lectures

"*The Pretense of Knowledge*" *Friedrich von Hayek* This highly readable essay explains the foolhardiness of economic planning
http://www.nobelprize.org/nobel_prizes/economics/laureates/1974/hayek-lecture.html

Capitalism and Freedom Milton Friedman (1962), highly influential series of essays that established Friedman's position on major issues of public policy.

Friedrich Hayek, *Individualism and Economic Order*, Chicago University Press, 1948.

Kelleher, William J.. *Progressive Logic: Framing A Unified Field Theory of Values For Progressives*. The Empathic Science Institute, 2005. ISBN 0-9773717-1-9

Kloppenberg, James T.. *Uncertain Victory: Social Democracy and Progressivism in European and American Thought, 1870-1920*. Oxford University Press, USA, 1988. ISBN 0-19-505304-4

Link, Arthur S. and McCormick, Richard L.. *Progressivism (American History Series)*. Harlan Davidson, 1983. ISBN 0-88295-814-3

McGerr, Michael *A Fierce Discontent: The Rise and Fall of the Progressive Movement in America, 1870-1920* (2003)

Marx, Karl and Friedrich Engels. *Communist Manifesto*. (Mass Market Paperback – REPRINT), Signet Classics, 1998. ISBN 978-0-451-52710-3

Mill, John Stuart (1844). "On the Definition of Political Economy; and on the Method of Investigation Proper to It"
Essays on Some Unsettled Questions of Political Economy.

Milton Friedman, Anna Jacobson Schwartz, (1971). *Monetary History of the United States, 1867–1960.* Princeton, N.J: Princeton University Press. ISBN 0-691-00354-

Say, Jean-Baptiste (1803). *A Treatise on Political Economy; or the Production, Distribution, and Consumption of Wealth*, trans. 1834,
Smith, Adam (1776). *An Inquiry into the Nature and Causes of the Wealth of Nations.*

The Road to Serfdom, Friedrich Hayek, Chicago University Press, 1944

Thomas Sowell *Basic Economics: A Common Sense Guide to the Economy. Third Edition,* Basic Books A member of the Perseus Book Group (2007) ISBN 13-978-0-465-00260-3

Williams, Walter E. (December 1, 2010d). *"Minimum Wage, Maximum Folly"*. Creators Syndicate. Archived from the original on February 9, 2011.

Williams, Walter E. (April 14, 2010a). *"Minimum wage cruelty"*. Creators Syndicate. Archived from the original on July 30, 2010.

Williams, Walter E. (March 24, 2005). "Minimum Wage Is Not An Anti-Poverty Tool". Investors Business Daily. Archived from the original on August 2, 2010. Retrieved December 8, 2010.

Williams, Walter E. (July 12, 2017). *"Minimum wage cruelty"*. Creators Syndicate. Retrieved June 3, 2020.

About the author

Mr. Moon had a long business career dealing with the major automotive manufacturers in Detroit, Michigan. He later created his own Sales and Marketing Company, expanding into industries including shipping, container makers, publishing, and recycling. This book is the result of years dealing with great and small markets. He has an A.B. from Syracuse University. Currently, he teaches and has authored books ranging from a military memoir to youth stories and textbooks.

Made in the USA
Monee, IL
03 November 2026

67387171R00105